Generating Kingdom Momentum

How Evangel Dean Catalysts Can Multiply Churches around the World

. . . .

Rev. Bob Engel
Rev. Dr. Don L. Davis

TUMI Press
3701 East Thirteenth Street North
Wichita, Kansas 67208

Generating Kingdom Momentum:
How Evangel Dean Catalysts Can Multiply Churches around the World

© 2019. The Urban Ministry Institute. All Rights Reserved.

The Urban Ministry Institute
3701 East 13th Street North
Wichita, KS 67208

ISBN: 978-1-62932-323-7

Published by TUMI Press
A division of World Impact, Inc.

The Urban Ministry Institute is a ministry of World Impact, Inc.

Table of Contents

Appendix

Welcome Letter

Greetings in the strong name of Jesus Christ!

The work of the Lord continues to gain momentum around the world today. Even though we face a harvest field that is more abundant and vast than ever before, the power and leading of the Holy Spirit spurs thousands of church planters, missionaries, evangelists, and Christian workers to share the Gospel of grace with the lost. Only the Spirit can supply us with the unction, anointing, and endowed gifts to make us successful in obeying our Savior's command to go to the ends of the earth with the Father's message of hope. In our estimation, your calling and availability are essential for these critical times. The harvest is plentiful and the workers continue to be few. As a Dean Catalyst of the Evangel movement, we are convinced that the Lord can and will use you to give birth to church planting movements who will deploy called, gifted, and totally surrendered workers into every city, town, and village.

Our invitation to you has been based on our full confidence that our Savior, the Lord of the harvest, has outfitted you to empower God-called leaders who in partnership with local churches will reach entire cities with the Gospel. It is the power of God for salvation to all who believe; in that simple Gospel God provides us with hope in this world and the world to come.

Our sincere prayer is that you will recognize your gifting and this opportunity. We are convinced that the Father will raise up dozens of Dean Catalysts who will equip deans in the far flung regions of this world, equipping men and women who have nurtured an apostolic heart, and who will give themselves without condition or qualification to reaching every boy, girl, woman, and man in the places to which God has called them. Our orientation for you, using this book, will underscore this vision and hopefully prepare you for your amazing journey ahead. Have no fear; God will refresh, challenge, and strengthen you as you equip deans and coaches to lead church planters among the forgotten poor.

Thank you for your love and commitment to Jesus Christ, the one who sacrificed everything to win to Christ a people for God. Join us as we seek to display the beauty of the Lord in loving, healthy assemblies planted among the broken, representing his Kingdom. May God grant us favor as we do all we can to obey the command of the Lord of the harvest, to bring in the plentiful harvest of God.

". . . Not of those who shrink back . . ." (Heb. 10.39)

Rev. Dr. Don Davis
Rev. Bob Engel

Generating Kingdom Momentum
How Evangel Dean Catalysts Can Multiply Churches around the World

Rev. Bob Engel, Rev. Dr. Don L. Davis

P – Partner in Mission

a. We affirm our global partnership with you to advance the mission of Christ by multiplying laborers for the harvest field.

b. We affirm our mutual love and honor for the Church; the steward of the Gospel of Jesus Christ.

c. We affirm our trust in you as a faithful co-laborer in the Gospel of Jesus Christ for the multiplying of laborers for the harvest field.

A – Ambassador for the TUMI Network

a. As an Ambassador of the TUMI Network we expect you to be aggressive in the multiplying of laborers who can proclaim the Good news, make disciples, identify and equip leaders, and establish new churches for the glory of God.

b. You will be representing the TUMI Network as the TUMI Network commits its resources, abilities, and calling to multiply laborers from and for the poor to proclaim the Gospel of the Kingdom to every people group.

c. Ambassadors of the TUMI Network are expected to be faithful to the procedures and commitments expected as a certified Evangel Dean Catalyst.

C – Certification privileges for an Evangel Dean Catalyst

a. As a certified Evangel Dean Catalyst you have the rights and authority to facilitate the *Evangel School of Urban Church Planting, Dean Training.*

b. As an Evangel Dean Catalyst you will represent Evangel and the TUMI Network through the use of the Evangel Logo and Evangel Dean curriculum and resources.

    c.   Evangel Dean Catalyst's are certified for three years with the opportunity to renew depending on the mutual agreement with the Head Dean.

K – Person who will advance the Kingdom

    a.   We expect Evangel Dean Catalysts to be Kingdom minded, driven and led by the Holy Spirit. The Kingdom is bigger than World Impact, the TUMI Network and your denomination.

    b.   The TUMI Network's Global Ends Statement encapsulates this Kingdom advancement: *The Gospel of the Kingdom proclaimed by the empowered urban poor to every people group through indigenous churches and movements.* As we represent this we expect our Evangel Dean Catalysts to represent this as well.

    c.   Advancing the Kingdom cannot be done by one's might, knowledge, or resources. Though we recognize these as coming from God, and will use them, we believe that Kingdom advancement and bearing fruit that will last is foundationally built upon one's abiding in Christ through the Holy Spirit.

S – Survey* and collect data on what the Holy Spirit is doing among those who are planting churches and winning people to Christ.

    a.   Number of churches chartered

    b.   Number of Gospel presentations made

    c.   Number of people who have responded to Christ

    d.   Number of churches planted

    e.   Number of Dean's commissioned

*Complete Dean Superintendent Report form quarterly: *www.tumi.org/deancatalyst*

Benefits

a. Belong to the TUMI Network, which connects those who share our passion for equipping Christian leaders and movements among the poor for the Great Commission

b. Authorized to host Evangel Dean Schools with Evangel resources in their ministry contexts, training others to certify church plant teams

c. Right to translate materials needed to host events and trainings as long as they correspond with TUMI's project protocols and systems (see *Translation Partnership Agreement SAMPLE* in Appendix)

d. If funding and opportunity is available, attend Evangel Gathering and pre-meeting

e. Evangel School of Urban Church Planting, Dean Training, certification card

f. Quarterly Cohort Meeting (ZOOM)

Appendix

The Nicene Creed with Biblical Support

The Urban Ministry Institute

We believe in one God,
> (Deut. 6.4-5; Mark 12.29; 1 Cor. 8.6)

the Father Almighty,
> (Gen. 17.1; Dan. 4.35; Matt. 6.9; Eph. 4.6; Rev. 1.8)

Maker of heaven and earth
> (Gen. 1.1; Isa. 40.28; Rev. 10.6)

and of all things visible and invisible.
> (Ps. 148; Rom. 11.36; Rev. 4.11)

We believe in one Lord Jesus Christ, the only Begotten Son of God, begotten of the Father before all ages, God from God, Light from Light, True God from True God, begotten not created, of the same essence as the Father,
> (John 1.1-2; 3.18; 8.58; 14.9-10; 20.28; Col. 1.15, 17; Heb. 1.3-6)

through whom all things were made.
> (John 1.3; Col. 1.16)

Who for us men and for our salvation came down from heaven and was incarnate by the Holy Spirit and the Virgin Mary and became human.
> (Matt. 1.20-23; John 1.14; 6.38; Luke 19.10)

Who for us too, was crucified under Pontius Pilate, suffered and was buried.
> (Matt. 27.1-2; Mark 15.24-39, 43-47; Acts 13.29; Rom. 5.8; Heb. 2.10; 13.12)

The third day he rose again according to the Scriptures,
> (Mark 16.5-7; Luke 24.6-8; Acts 1.3; Rom. 6.9; 10.9; 2 Tim. 2.8)

ascended into heaven, and is seated at the right hand of the Father.
> (Mark 16.19; Eph. 1.19-20)

He will come again in glory to judge the living and the dead, and his Kingdom will have no end.
> (Isa. 9.7; Matt. 24.30; John 5.22; Acts 1.11; 17.31; Rom. 14.9; 2 Cor. 5.10; 2 Tim. 4.1)

We believe in the Holy Spirit, the Lord and life-giver,
> *(Gen. 1.1-2; Job 33.4; Ps. 104.30; 139.7-8; Luke 4.18-19; John 3.5-6; Acts 1.1-2; 1 Cor. 2.11; Rev. 3.22)*

who proceeds from the Father and the Son,
> *(John 14.16-18, 26; 15.26; 20.22)*

who together with the Father and Son is worshiped and glorified,
> *(Isa. 6.3; Matt. 28.19; 2 Cor. 13.14; Rev. 4.8)*

who spoke by the prophets.
> *(Num. 11.29; Mic. 3.8; Acts 2.17-18; 2 Pet. 1.21)*

We believe in one holy, catholic, and apostolic Church.
> *(Matt. 16.18; Eph. 5.25-28; 1 Cor. 1.2; 10.17; 1 Tim. 3.15; Rev. 7.9)*

We acknowledge one baptism for the forgiveness of sin,
> *(Acts 22.16; 1 Pet. 3.21; Eph. 4.4-5)*

And we look for the resurrection of the dead and the life of the age to come.
> *(Isa. 11.6-10; Mic. 4.1-7; Luke 18.29-30; Rev. 21.1-5; 21.22-22.5)*

Amen.

The Nicene Creed with Biblical Support – Memory Verses

Below are suggested memory verses, one for each section of the Creed.

The Father
Rev. 4.11 – Worthy are you, our Lord and God, to receive glory and honor and power, for you created all things, and by your will they existed and were created.

The Son
John 1.1 – In the beginning was the Word, and the Word was with God, and the Word was God.

The Son's Mission
1 Cor. 15.3-5 – For what I received I passed on to you as of first importance: that Christ died for our sins according to the Scriptures, that he was buried, that he was raised on the third day according to the Scriptures, and that he appeared to Peter, and then to the Twelve.

The Holy Spirit
Rom. 8.11 – If the Spirit of him who raised Jesus from the dead dwells in you, he who raised Christ Jesus from the dead will also give life to your mortal bodies through his Spirit who dwells in you.

The Church

1 Pet. 2.9 – But you are a chosen race, a royal priesthood, a holy nation, a people for his own possession, that you may proclaim the excellencies of him who called you out of darkness into his marvelous light.

Our Hope

1 Thess. 4.16-17 – For the Lord himself will descend from heaven with a cry of command, with the voice of an archangel, and with the sound of the trumpet of God. And the dead in Christ will rise first. Then we who are alive, who are left, will be caught up together with them in the clouds to meet the Lord in the air, and so we will always be with the Lord.

World Impact's Mission Statement and Global Ends Statement

Our Mission Statement
World Impact empowers urban leaders and partners with local churches to reach their cities with the Gospel.

Our Global Ends Statement
The Gospel of the Kingdom proclaimed by the empowered urban poor to every people group through indigenous churches and movements

Representing God:
Living as an Emissary of the Most High

Rev. Dr. Don L. Davis

On the Two Kinds of Pretense
(C.S. Lewis on the Lord's Prayer)

It's very first words are *Our Father* Do you now see what those words mean? They mean quite frankly, that you are putting yourself in the place of a son of God. To put it bluntly, you are dressing up as Christ. If you like, you are pretending. Because, of course, the moment you realize what the words mean, you realize that you are not a son of God. You are not being like *The* Son of God, whose will and interests are at one with those of the Father: you are a bundle of self-centered fears, hopes, greeds, jealousies, and self-conceit, all doomed to death. So that, in a way, this dressing up as Christ is a piece of outrageous cheek. But the odd thing is that He has ordered us to do it.

Why? What is the good of pretending to be what you are not? Well, even on the human level, you know, there are two kinds of pretending. There is a *bad kind*, where the *pretense is there instead of the real thing*; as when a man pretends he is going to help you instead of really helping you. But there is also a *good kind*, where *the pretense leads up to the real thing* [italics mine].

When you are not feeling particularly friendly but know you ought to be, the best thing you can do, very often, is to put on a friendly manner and behave as if you were a nicer person than you actually are. And in a few minutes, as we have all noticed, you will be really feeling friendlier than you were. Very often the only way to get a quality in reality is to start behaving as if you had it already. That is why children's games are so important. They are *always pretending to be grown-ups* – playing soldiers, playing shop. But all the time, they are hardening their muscles and sharpening their wits, so that the pretense of being grown-up helps them to grow up in earnest.

~ C. S. Lewis. *Mere Christianity*.
New York: Macmilliam Publishing Company, 1943, copyright renewed © 1980.
pp. 162-63.

The Golden Rule of Good Pretense

Act every day like *what you been told you is*,
cause' if you fail to act just like *what you really be*,
then you'll never become *what you have been from the beginnin'*!

Representing God:
Living as an Emissary
of the Most High,
continued

Understand the *definition* of representation, follow the *dynamics* of representation, persevere through the *difficulties* of representation, and adopt the *demeanor* of representation.

I. Understand the Definition of Representation

A. Representation as a concept

"To represent another is to be selected to stand in the place of another, and thereby fulfill the assigned duties, exercise the rights and serve as deputy for, as well as to speak and act with another's authority on behalf of their interests and reputation."

Representation is essentially the process of investing, empowering, and assessing for results (see Appendix).

1. *Apostleship* as representation

a. *Apostolos* (apostle): "one who is sent out by another," cf. Acts 1.2, 26; 6.2; 8.1; 14.4, 14; cf. 1 Cor. 12.28-29

b. Apostles are not volunteers – they are called by selection to represent the sender, Rom. 1.1; Acts 1.25; 1 Cor. 9.2

c. Apostles are called to suffer, 1 Cor. 4.9ff.; 2 Cor. 11;

d. Apostles authenticate their calling through their deeds and words

(1) The original apostles saw the risen Lord, 1 Cor. 9.1; 15.7-9; Acts 1.21-22

(2) Believers are converted and churches planted through their work, 1 Cor. 9.1-2

(3) They perform signs, wonders, and miracles in the power of the Spirit, 2 Cor. 12.12

(4) They laid the foundation for the church through their ministries, writings, and prayers, Eph. 2.20; 2 Pet. 3.2

2. *Evangelist, herald* (messengers) as representation

*Representing God:
Living as an Emissary
of the Most High,*
continued

a. *Evanggelistes* (evangelist): "someone who brings good news," Acts 21.8; Eph. 4.11; 2 Tim. 4.5

b. *Keryx* (herald): "denotes the person who is commissioned by his ruler or the state to call out with a clear voice some item of news and so to make it known" (David Bennett, *Metaphors of Ministry*, p. 135); cf. 1 Tim. 2.7; 2 Tim. 1.11

c. Both *evangellos* and *keryx* presuppose the delivery of a message on behalf of someone else (neither were allowed to make up their own announcements; *faithful proclamation* lies at the heart of their duties)

3. *Ambassadorship* as representation

a. *Presbeuo* (to be an authorized representative, to be an ambassador or do the work of an ambassador), 2 Cor. 5.20

b. Speaks as though God was making his own appeal *through them*, 2 Cor. 5.20

c. Paul considered himself an "ambassador in chains," Eph. 6.20

d. "As a prisoner in Rome, to which foreign delegates came from far and wide, Paul thinks of himself as an ambassador from the King of kings. The status of the ambassador is generally related to the status of the rule that he represents. This high honor is therefore a privilege available to the humblest of willing believers" (David Bennett, *Metaphors of Ministry*, p. 136).

B. Jesus as the perfect representative of God

Luke 10.1 – After this *the Lord appointed seventy-two others and sent them on ahead of him*, two by two, into every town and place where he himself was about to go.

Luke 10.16 – "The one who *hears you hears me*, and the one who *rejects you rejects me*, and the one who *rejects me rejects him who sent me*."

Representing God:
Living as an Emissary
of the Most High,
continued

John 20.21 – Jesus said to them again, "Peace be with you. *As the Father has sent me, even so I am sending you."*

1. Jesus fulfills the duties of being the emissary of God (see appendix *Representin': Jesus as God's Chosen Representative*)

    a. He received an assignment from the Father, John 10.17-18.

    b. He was empowered by God's entrustment of the Holy Spirit, John 3.34; Luke 4.18.

    c. He engaged in the mission with wholeheartedly and unreserved obedience, John 5.30.

    d. He was judged by the One who sent him to be faithful and true, Matt. 3.16-17.

    e. He fulfilled his task with perfect compliance with the Father's will, even to the point of death, Phil. 2.5-8.

    f. He was exalted and rewarded by God as a result of his faithful commission with never ending glory and honor, Phil. 2.9-11.

2. Revealed in his life and ministry

    a. The Baptism of Jesus: the commissioning and confirmation of God's representative, Mark 1.9-11

    b. The Temptations of Jesus: the challenge presented to God's representative, Mark 1.12-13

    c. The Public Ministry of Jesus: communication and display of God's representative, Mark 1.14-15

    d. *Understanding Leadership as Representation: The Six Stages of Formal Proxy* (see Appendix)

*Representing God:
Living as an Emissary
of the Most High*,
continued

"You Got to Serve Somebody!"

Over half of the metaphors chosen by Jesus describe someone who is under the authority of another. Often the word selected is one member of a familiar role pair, such as child (of a father, *pater*), servant (of a master, *kyrios*), or disciple (of a teacher, *didaskalos*). Other images of those under authority include the shepherd (*poimen*) who tends a flock that belongs to another, the worker (*ergates*) hired by the landowner (*oikodespotes*), the apostle (*apostolos*) commissioned by his superior, and the sheep (*probaton*) obeying the voice of the shepherd. It is interesting to note that even though the disciples are being prepared for spiritual leadership in the Church, Jesus places far more emphasis on their responsibility to God's authority, than on the authority which they themselves will exercise. There is far more instruction about the role of *following* than about the role of *leading*.

~ David Bennett. *The Metaphors of Ministry*. p. 62

II. Follow the Dynamics of Representation

The following dynamics constitute the active stages and actions involved in every assignment of responsibility for an emissary, envoy, or representative. A representative is one who receives a mandate, one who is sent somewhere to say and do something for someone who empowers them to speak and act on their behalf. These dynamics form the body of the actual act of delegation to a representative, and through them we can understand both the phases and styles of representative leadership.

A. *The Commissioning*: a representative receives a formal selection and call to represent.

   1. An emissary is *chosen* to be an envoy or proxy.

   2. This selection is confirmed both by the sender and the one sent; it is neither arbitrary or self-determined.

   3. The call is a commission to something: *to a particular position, task, or mission*.

   4. The call includes both *privilege* and *responsibility*.

Representing God:
Living as an Emissary
of the Most High,
continued

5. An authentic call is *backed up by legitimate authority and right to act on behalf of the sender.*

6. *The Pauline example*: the call of the Damascus Road, Acts 9

    a. Acts 9.15-16 – *But the Lord said to him, "Go, for he is a chosen instrument of mine to carry my name before the Gentiles and kings and the children of Israel. [16] For I will show him how much he must suffer for the sake of my name."*

    b. Acts 22.7-10, 21 – "And I fell to the ground and heard a voice saying to me, 'Saul, Saul, why are you persecuting me?' [8] And I answered, 'Who are you, Lord?' And he said to me, 'I am Jesus of Nazareth, whom you are persecuting.' [9] Now those who were with me saw the light but did not understand the voice of the one who was speaking to me. [10] And I said, 'What shall I do, Lord?' And the Lord said to me, 'Rise, and go into Damascus, and there you will be told all that is appointed for you to do.' [21] And he said to me, 'Go, for I will send you far away to the Gentiles.'"

B. *The Equipping*: a representative receives appropriate training and resources to fulfill the call

    1. A representative is an emissary: s/he is assigned to go somewhere, do something, or fulfill some task.

    2. The task presupposes equipping and resourcing to accomplish the work.

    3. Training + gifting + support + opportunity + disciplined effort = equipping

    4. The importance of mentorship and coaching

    5. *The Pauline example*: the retreat into Arabia, Gal. 1.13-24 – For you have heard of my former life in Judaism, how I persecuted the church of God violently and tried to destroy it. [14] And I was advancing in Judaism beyond many of my own age among my people, so extremely zealous was I for the traditions of my fathers. [15] *But when he who had set me apart before I was born, and who called me by his grace, [16] was pleased to reveal his Son to me, in order that I might preach him among the Gentiles, I did not immediately consult with*

*Representing God:
Living as an Emissary
of the Most High,*
continued

anyone; [17] nor did I go up to Jerusalem to those who were apostles before me, but I went away into Arabia, and returned again to Damascus. [18] **Then after three years I went up to Jerusalem to visit Cephas and remained with him fifteen days.** [19] But I saw none of the other apostles except James the Lord's brother. [20] (In what I am writing to you, before God, I do not lie!) [21] Then I went into the regions of Syria and Cilicia. [22] And I was still unknown in person to the churches of Judea that are in Christ. [23] They only were hearing it said, "He who used to persecute us is now preaching the faith he once tried to destroy." [24] And they glorified God because of me.

C. *The Entrustment*: a representative is endowed with the authority and power to act on behalf of the sender

1. The sender delegates to the representative the authority to speak and act on his/her behalf.

2. The scope and limits of the authority must be carefully delineated.

3. Usually in a public and/or official ceremony, the emissary is sworn and/or deputized with the authority to represent.

4. With this confirmation, the representative now officially is given the right to represent and released to do the task.

5. *The Pauline example*: the display of signs, wonders, and miracles of the Holy Spirit in the act of proclaiming Christ as Messiah, Rom. 15.15-21 – But on some points I have written to you very boldly by way of reminder, *because of the grace given me by God [16] to be a minister of Christ Jesus to the Gentiles in the priestly service of the gospel of God, so that the offering of the Gentiles may be acceptable, sanctified by the Holy Spirit.* [17] In Christ Jesus, then, I have reason to be proud of my work for God. [18] *For I will not venture to speak of anything except what Christ has accomplished through me to bring the Gentiles to obedience – by word and deed, [19] by the power of signs and wonders, by the power of the Spirit of God – so that from Jerusalem and all the way around to Illyricum I have fulfilled the ministry of the gospel of Christ;* [20] and thus I make it my ambition to preach the gospel, not where Christ has already been named, lest I build on someone else's foundation, [21] but as it is written, "Those who have never

Representing God:
Living as an Emissary
of the Most High,
continued

been told of him will see, and those who have never heard will understand."

D. *The Mission*: a representative faithfully and with great discipline engages the task.

1. A representative *subordinates* his/her will in order to fulfill the task.

2. Obedience is the mark of a faithful representative.

3. The key virtues of a representative: loyalty, integrity, and wholehearted engagement.

4. The mission is about *achieving results*, not about *possessing intentions*.

5. *The Pauline example*: the evangelization of the Roman world, Col. 1:21-23 (ESV) And you, who once were alienated and hostile in mind, doing evil deeds, [22] he has now reconciled in his body of flesh by his death, in order to present you holy and blameless and above reproach before him, [23] if indeed you continue in the faith, stable and steadfast, not shifting from the hope of the gospel that you heard, *which has been proclaimed in all creation under heaven, and of which I, Paul, became a minister.*

E. *The Reckoning*: a representative is answerable to the one who sent him/her.

1. A representative reports back to the sending authority for evaluation and review

2. The review is formal, comprehensive, and decisive

3. Both the *work product* and *personal predisposition during the work* are evaluated

4. The Pauline example: the Bema Seat of Christ

   a. Paul as a minister accountable to the Lord for his work, 1 Cor. 3.5-9 – *What then is Apollos? What is Paul? Servants through whom you believed, as the Lord assigned to each. [6] I planted, Apollos watered, but God gave the growth.*

*Representing God:
Living as an Emissary
of the Most High,*
continued

[7] So neither he who plants nor he who waters is anything, but only God who gives the growth. [8] He who plants and he who waters are one, and each will receive his wages according to his labor. [9] For we are God's fellow workers. You are God's field, God's building.

b. The coming assessment of the quality of our works before the One who gave us our mandate

(1) 1 Cor. 3.10-15 – According to the grace of God given to me, like a skilled master builder I laid a foundation, and someone else is building upon it. *Let each one take care how he builds upon it. [11] For no one can lay a foundation other than that which is laid, which is Jesus Christ. [12] Now if anyone builds on the foundation with gold, silver, precious stones, wood, hay, straw – [13] each one's work will become manifest, for the Day will disclose it, because it will be revealed by fire,* and the fire will test what sort of work each one has done. [14] If the work that anyone has built on the foundation survives, he will receive a reward. [15] If anyone's work is burned up, he will suffer loss, though he himself will be saved, but only as through fire.

(2) 1 Cor. 4.2-5 – Moreover, it is required of stewards that they be found trustworthy. *[3] But with me it is a very small thing that I should be judged by you or by any human court. In fact, I do not even judge myself.* [4] I am not aware of anything against myself, but I am not thereby acquitted. It is the Lord who judges me. *[5] Therefore do not pronounce judgment before the time, before the Lord comes, who will bring to light the things now hidden in darkness and will disclose the purposes of the heart. Then each one will receive his commendation from God.*

F. *The Reward*: a representative is recognized and rewarded on the basis of his/her faithful representation of the sender

1. The results are formally assessed and often publicly acknowledged, whether good or bad

2. The sender acknowledges and recognizes the behavior, conduct, and product of the representative's actions

*Representing God:
Living as an Emissary
of the Most High,*
continued

3. The reward and recognition corresponds to the level of faithful obedience to the task

4. New levels of responsibility and authority are given depending on the level of faithful execution of the task

5. *The Pauline example*: the Crowns of Christ (symbol of authority, splendor, and glory)

    a. 1 Cor. 9.16-18 – For if I preach the gospel, that gives me no ground for boasting. For necessity is laid upon me. Woe to me if I do not preach the gospel! [17] *For if I do this of my own will, I have a reward, but not of my own will, I am still entrusted with a stewardship.*

    b. 1 Cor. 9.24-25 – Do you not know that in a race all the runners compete, but only one receives the prize? So run that you may obtain it. [25] Every athlete exercises self-control in all things. *They do it to receive a perishable wreath, but we an imperishable.*

    c. 2 Tim. 4.6-8 – For I am already being poured out as a drink offering, and the time of my departure has come. [7] I have fought the good fight, I have finished the race, I have kept the faith. [8] *Henceforth there is laid up for me the crown of righteousness, which the Lord, the righteous judge, will award to me on that Day, and not only to me but also to all who have loved his appearing.*

    d. 2 Tim. 2.5 – *An athlete is not crowned unless he competes according to the rules.*

    e. James 1.12 – Blessed is the man who remains steadfast under trial, for *when he has stood the test he will receive the crown of life*, which God has promised to those who love him.

    f. 1 Peter 5.4 – And *when the chief Shepherd appears, you will receive the unfading crown of glory.*

    g. Rev. 2.10 – Do not fear what you are about to suffer. Behold, the devil is about to throw some of you into prison, that you may be tested, and for ten days you will have tribulation. *Be faithful unto death, and I will give you the crown of life.*

*Representing God:
Living as an Emissary
of the Most High,*
continued

6. *Understanding Leadership as Representation: The Six Stages of Formal Proxy* (see appendix)

III. Persevere through the Difficulties of Representation

A. The inward irritations: the difficulties of conscience, conviction, character

   1. The confidence of **conscience**: *What do you do when you reach a crisis of conscience in representing your sender?*, 1 Tim. 1.5 – The aim of our charge is love that issues from *a pure heart and a good conscience and a sincere faith.*

      a. Being asked to do something that gnaws against your conscience and ideas, i.e., sometimes not feeling good about what you're asked to do and be in the community

      b. Persistent doubt over a course of action that goes beyond mere conflict over ideas (a long-term issue or problem)

      c. Struggling with your submission period, i.e., feeling small because you are commanded to do things

   2. The clarity of **conviction**: *What do you do when your own personal belief system conflicts with what your sender wants you to do?*

      a. Scriptures

         (1) Rom. 14:5 – One person esteems one day as better than another, while another esteems all days alike. *Each one should be fully convinced in his own mind.*

         (2) Rom. 14:22-23 –The faith that you have, keep between yourself and God. *Blessed is the one who has no reason to pass judgment on himself for what he approves.* [23] But whoever has doubts is condemned if he eats, because the eating is not from faith. *For whatever does not proceed from faith is sin.*

      b. Being asked to do something that mildly goes against your own denominational practice and theology

Representing God:
Living as an Emissary
of the Most High,
continued

c. Wrestling with the dilemma of wanting to be hospitable to one's neighbors, yet guarding the influence of others on one family and children

d. Commanded to be silent on or allow for differences on things that previously were a big part of your own thinking and practice

e. Struggling with persistent doubt with the judgment and/or motives of one's leaders and/or superiors

f. Living in freedom in an inter-denominational setting regarding things that are different from your own denomination's views

3. The challenge of **character**: *How does one's character shape and affect the kind of representation that you offer to your sender?*

    a. Scripture: 2 Tim. 2.1-7 – You then, my child, be strengthened by the grace that is in Christ Jesus, [2] and what you have heard from me in the presence of many witnesses *entrust to faithful men who will be able to teach others also.* [3] *Share in suffering as a good soldier of Christ Jesus.* [4] *No soldier gets entangled in civilian pursuits,* since his aim is to please the one who enlisted him. [5] An athlete is not crowned *unless he competes according to the rules.* [6] It is *the hardworking farmer who ought to have the first share of the crops.* [7] Think over what I say, for the Lord will give you understanding in everything.

    b. Struggling with limited remuneration and salary compared to others of your age and profession

        (1) Only earning furniture that you buy and have to put together yourself, or came from a donation

        (2) Only driving cars that leak and sputter when they do run

        (3) Facing depression due to unbroken ministry fatigue and failure

        (4) Living in a community with people who do not want you there or like you very much

*Representing God:
Living as an Emissary
of the Most High,*
continued

(5) Wearing clothes that "completed the cycle": that were hip, went out of style, and now are back in style

(6) Living and working in facilities that are fatigued and difficult

4. Note: these difficulties are associated with internal issues impacting the representative's confidence

B. The outward obstacles: the difficulties of investment, empowerment, and assessment (see appendix *Investment, Empowerment, and Assessment*)

1. The lack of **investment**: *What do you do when you feel that you are given a task to do without the requisite investment prior to engaging it?*

   a. Scripture: Eph. 4.11-13 – And he gave the apostles, the prophets, the evangelists, the pastors and teachers, [12] to equip the saints for the work of ministry, for building up the body of Christ, [13] until we all attain to the unity of the faith and of the knowledge of the Son of God, to mature manhood, to the measure of the stature of the fullness of Christ.

   b. Having to make due with old, substandard, or broken equipment and gear

   c. No funds for training seminars and workshops to help grow your talent

   d. Operating on a shoestring budget all the time

2. The absence of **empowerment**: *What do you do when after engaging the task, you feel that you have neither the freedom nor the resources to carry out that mission?*

   a. Scriptures

      (1) Rom. 15.1 – We who are strong have an obligation to bear with the failings of the weak, and not to please ourselves.

Representing God:
Living as an Emissary
of the Most High,
continued

(2) Gal. 5.13-14 – For you were called to freedom, brothers. Only do not use your freedom as an opportunity for the flesh, but through love serve one another. [14] For the whole law is fulfilled in one word: "You shall love your neighbor as yourself."

(3) Gal. 6.2 – Bear one another's burdens, and so fulfill the law of Christ.

   b. Being confused about the authority you have to carry out a task

   c. Forming ad-hoc groups of people to do complex or difficult jobs

   d. Asked to work under people whose expertise and experience is less than your own

3. The irregularity of **assessment**: *What do you do when in the act of engaging the mission or afterwards you feel you did not get the proper feedback as to your performance?*

   a. Scriptures

      (1) 1 Thess. 5.14 – And we urge you, brothers, admonish the idle, encourage the fainthearted, help the weak, be patient with them all.

      (2) Gal. 6.5 – For each will have to bear his own load.

   b. Little or no feedback after what you take to be important jobs or projects

   c. Not being recognized for the sacrifice and effort you put into a job

   d. Feeling harshly criticized or judged after your performance in a ministry activity or event

4. Note: These difficulties are associated with *external issues* affecting the representative's performance.

C. *Leader-Follower Representations* (see appendix)

Representing God:
Living as an Emissary
of the Most High,
continued

IV. Adopt the Demeanor of Your Representation as an Evangel Dean Catalyst

A. Recognize your place *as an agent of the Lord*: affirm the significance of understanding leadership as representation.

   1. *Jesus was a representative of the Father* who fulfilled with perfect obedience and flawless accuracy precisely what the Father wanted him to do, Phil. 2.5-8.

   2. *Jesus appointed the apostles as representatives of himself*, even as he was a representative of the Father, John 20.

   3. *You are now a part of the sacred tapestry of leadership as representation*: the authority of the risen Lord continues to be dispensed among the members of the church for his purposes, Eph. 1.19-23.

B. Adjust your persona when you are acting as a Dean Catalyst (match your demeanor with your designation).

   1. *Get your pretense on!* Do not be colloquial or causal about your acceptance as a Dean Catalyst; you will be *formally* acknowledged, *formally* accepted, *formally* commissioned, and *formally* assigned your place

   2. Embrace your identity as *a representative of the Church, as a minister of your own movement, and an agent of Evangel*. During that assignment, you are called to represent both the Gospel and our network now in all you do (your words, disposition, attitude, communication, etc.)

   3. *Commit to excellence in knowing the principles, policies, and protocols of the Evangel Dean process*. Your representation will be no better than your informed, committed, and focused application of the Evangel vision and direction.

      a. You are now called *to represent the Kingdom of God* as an apostle of the Lord for global missions.

      b. You are *an agent of the Gospel for leveraging multiplying laborers aggressively in the most unreached peoples and communities we know of* (with all the privileges, responsibilities, and stigmas associated with it thereto!)

C. As you begin to share your Dean Catalyst calling, *embrace your identity as a deputy and emissary of the World Impact community.*

1. Represent the purposes, priorities, and policies of World Impact's Evangel School of Urban Church Planting clearly and passionately; *be professional and dignified.*

2. Differentiate between your opinion and WI vision or Evangel policy: *do not misspeak.*

3. *Recognize your official status as you begin your Dean Catalyst representation.* Give yourself time to grow into your new identity as a representative of the Gospel of Jesus Christ, affiliated through the Evangel Dean School of Urban Church Planting of World Impact.

• Recall the definition of representation
• Follow the dynamics of representation
• Persevere through the difficulties of representation
• Adopt the demeanor of representation

The Bottom Line: Remember Lewis's *good kind* of pretending, where *the pretense leads up to the real thing.*

Now, by faith and confirmation of the leaders of the Lord, you have been accepted as an emissary of the Most High God, and a Evangel Dean Catalyst! May you be faithful to live out before others what you truly are!

APPENDIX 4

Representin': Jesus as God's Chosen Representative

Rev. Dr. Don L. Davis

To represent another
Is to be selected to stand in the place of another, and thereby fulfill the assigned duties, exercise the rights and serve as deputy for, as well as to speak and act with another's authority on behalf of their interests and reputation.

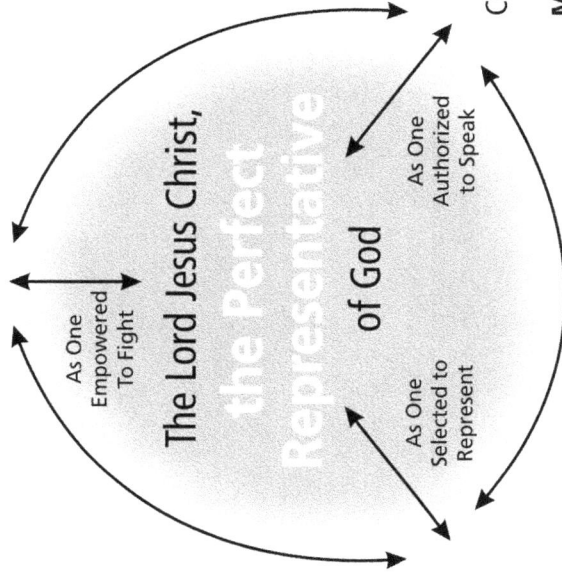

The Temptation of Jesus Christ
Challenge to and Contention with God's Rep

Mark 1.12-13 – The Spirit immediately drove him out into the wilderness. [13] *And he was in the wilderness forty days, being tempted by Satan.* And he was with the wild animals, and the angels were ministering to him.

The Public Preaching Ministry of Jesus Christ
Communication and Conveyance by God's Rep

Mark 1.14-15 – Now after John was arrested, Jesus came into Galilee, proclaiming the gospel of God, and saying, "The time is fulfilled, and the kingdom of God is at hand; repent and believe in the gospel."

The Lord Jesus Christ, the Perfect Representative of God

As One Empowered To Fight

As One Authorized to Speak

As One Selected to Represent

Jesus Fulfills The Duties Of Being an Emissary

1. Receiving an *Assignment,*
   John 10.17-18

2. Resourced with an *Entrustment,*
   John 3.34; Luke. 4.18

3. Launched into *Engagement,*
   John 5.30

4. Answered with an *Assessment,*
   Matthew 3.16-17

5. New assignment after *Assessment,*
   Philippians 2.9-11

The Baptism of Jesus Christ
Commissioning and Confirmation of God's Rep

Mark 1.9-11 – *In those days Jesus came from Nazareth of Galilee and was baptized by John in the Jordan.* [10] And when he came up out of the water, immediately he saw the heavens opening and the Spirit descending on him like a dove. [11] And a voice came from heaven, "You are my beloved Son; with you I am well pleased."

APPENDIX 5

Understanding Leadership as Representation: The Six Stages of Formal Proxy

Rev. Dr. Don L. Davis

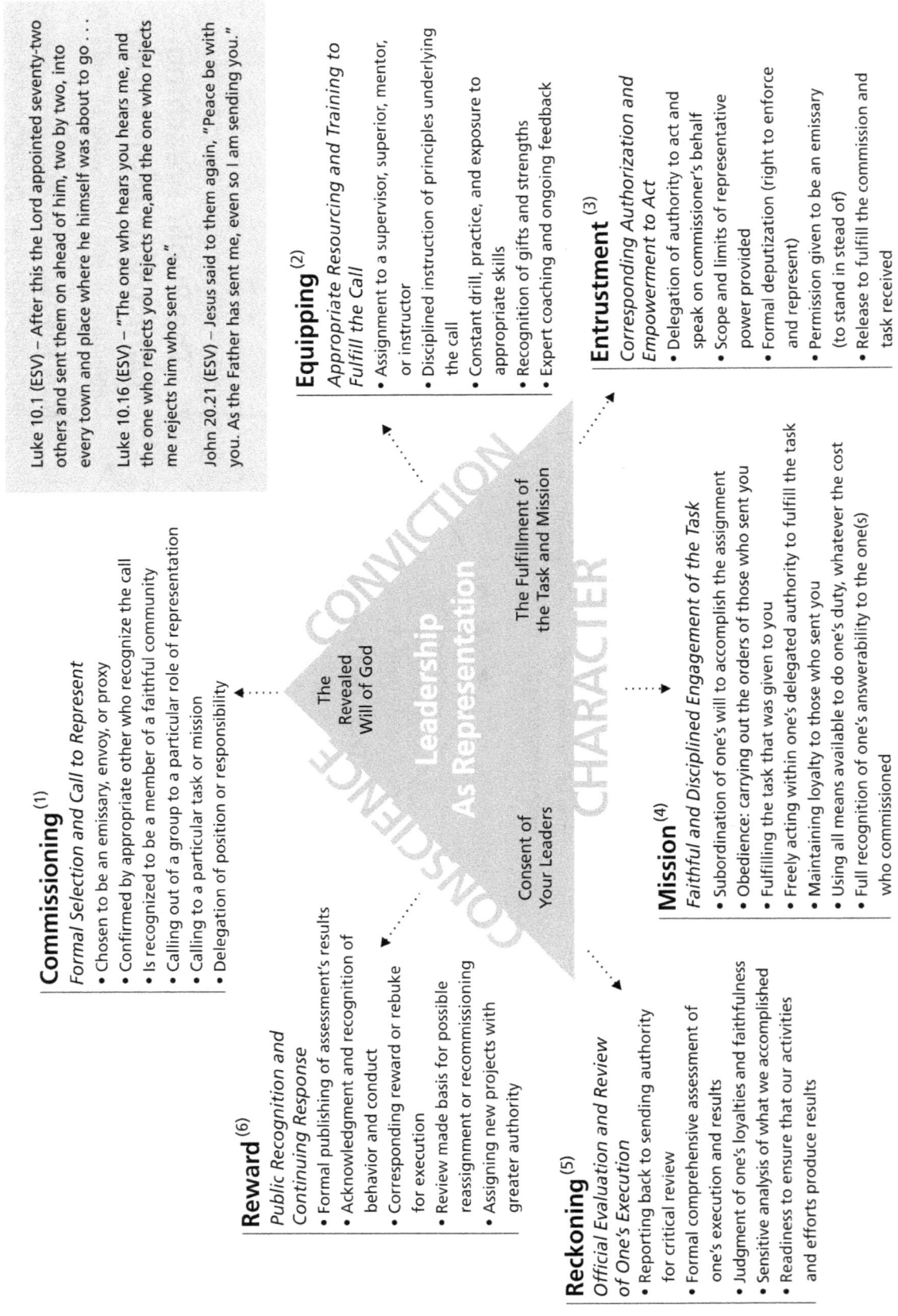

Luke 10.1 (ESV) – After this the Lord appointed seventy-two others and sent them on ahead of him, two by two, into every town and place where he himself was about to go . . . .

Luke 10.16 (ESV) – "The one who hears you hears me, and the one who rejects you rejects me, and the one who rejects me rejects him who sent me."

John 20.21 (ESV) – Jesus said to them again, "Peace be with you. As the Father has sent me, even so I am sending you."

Commissioning [1]
Formal Selection and Call to Represent
- Chosen to be an emissary, envoy, or proxy
- Confirmed by appropriate other who recognize the call
- Is recognized to be a member of a faithful community
- Calling out of a group to a particular role of representation
- Calling to a particular task or mission
- Delegation of position or responsibility

Equipping [2]
Appropriate Resourcing and Training to Fulfill the Call
- Assignment to a supervisor, superior, mentor, or instructor
- Disciplined instruction of principles underlying the call
- Constant drill, practice, and exposure to appropriate skills
- Recognition of gifts and strengths
- Expert coaching and ongoing feedback

Entrustment [3]
Corresponding Authorization and Empowerment to Act
- Delegation of authority to act and speak on commissioner's behalf
- Scope and limits of representative power provided
- Formal deputization (right to enforce and represent)
- Permission given to be an emissary (to stand in stead of)
- Release to fulfill the commission and task received

CONVICTION

CONSCIENCE

CHARACTER

Leadership As Representation

The Revealed Will of God

The Fulfillment of the Task and Mission

Consent of Your Leaders

Mission [4]
Faithful and Disciplined Engagement of the Task
- Subordination of one's will to accomplish the assignment
- Obedience: carrying out the orders of those who sent you
- Fulfilling the task that was given to you
- Freely acting within one's delegated authority to fulfill the task
- Maintaining loyalty to those who sent you
- Using all means available to do one's duty, whatever the cost
- Full recognition of one's answerability to the one(s) who commissioned

Reckoning [5]
Official Evaluation and Review of One's Execution
- Reporting back to sending authority for critical review
- Formal comprehensive assessment of one's execution and results
- Judgment of one's loyalties and faithfulness
- Sensitive analysis of what we accomplished
- Readiness to ensure that our activities and efforts produce results

Reward [6]
Public Recognition and Continuing Response
- Formal publishing of assessment's results
- Acknowledgment and recognition of behavior and conduct
- Corresponding reward or rebuke for execution
- Review made basis for possible reassignment or recommissioning
- Assigning new projects with greater authority

APPENDIX 6

Leader/Follower Representations

Rev. Dr. Don L. Davis

What the Leader Provides

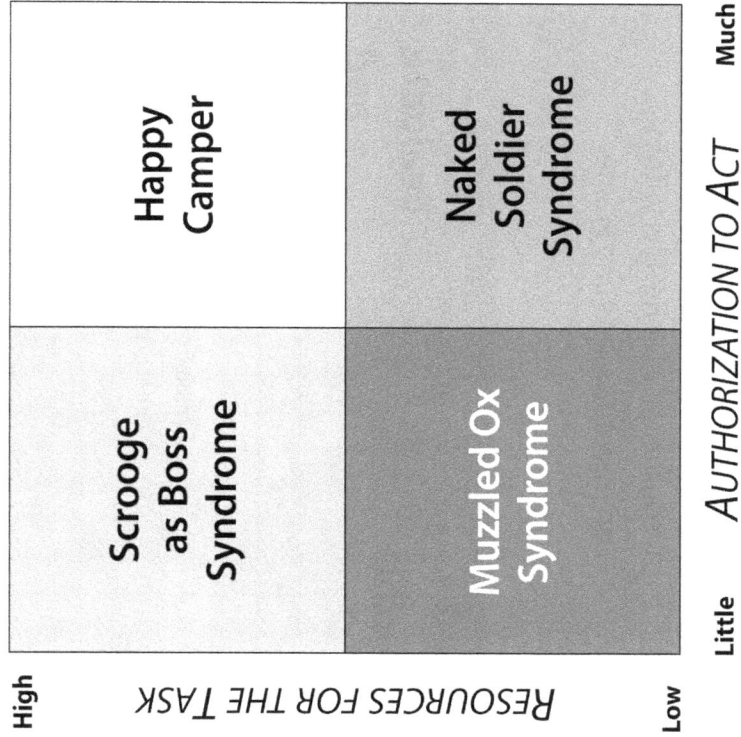

Scrooge as Boss Syndrome	**Happy Camper**	High
Muzzled Ox Syndrome	**Naked Soldier Syndrome**	Low
Little	Much	

RESOURCES FOR THE TASK

AUTHORIZATION TO ACT

What the Follower Expresses

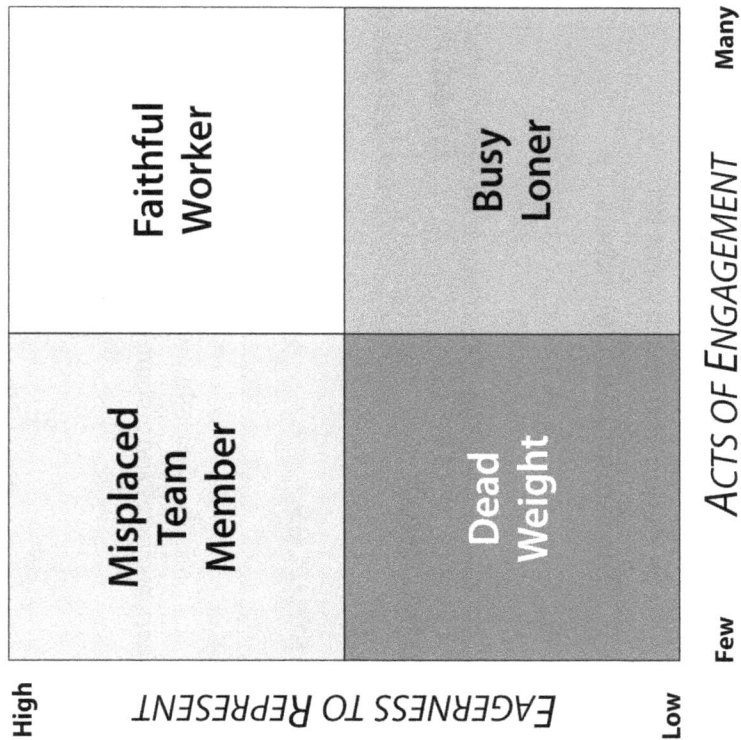

Misplaced Team Member	**Faithful Worker**	High
Dead Weight	**Busy Loner**	Low
Few	Many	

EAGERNESS TO REPRESENT

ACTS OF ENGAGEMENT

APPENDIX 7

Investment, Empowerment, and Assessment
How Leadership as Representation Provides Freedom to Innovate

Rev. Dr. Don L. Davis

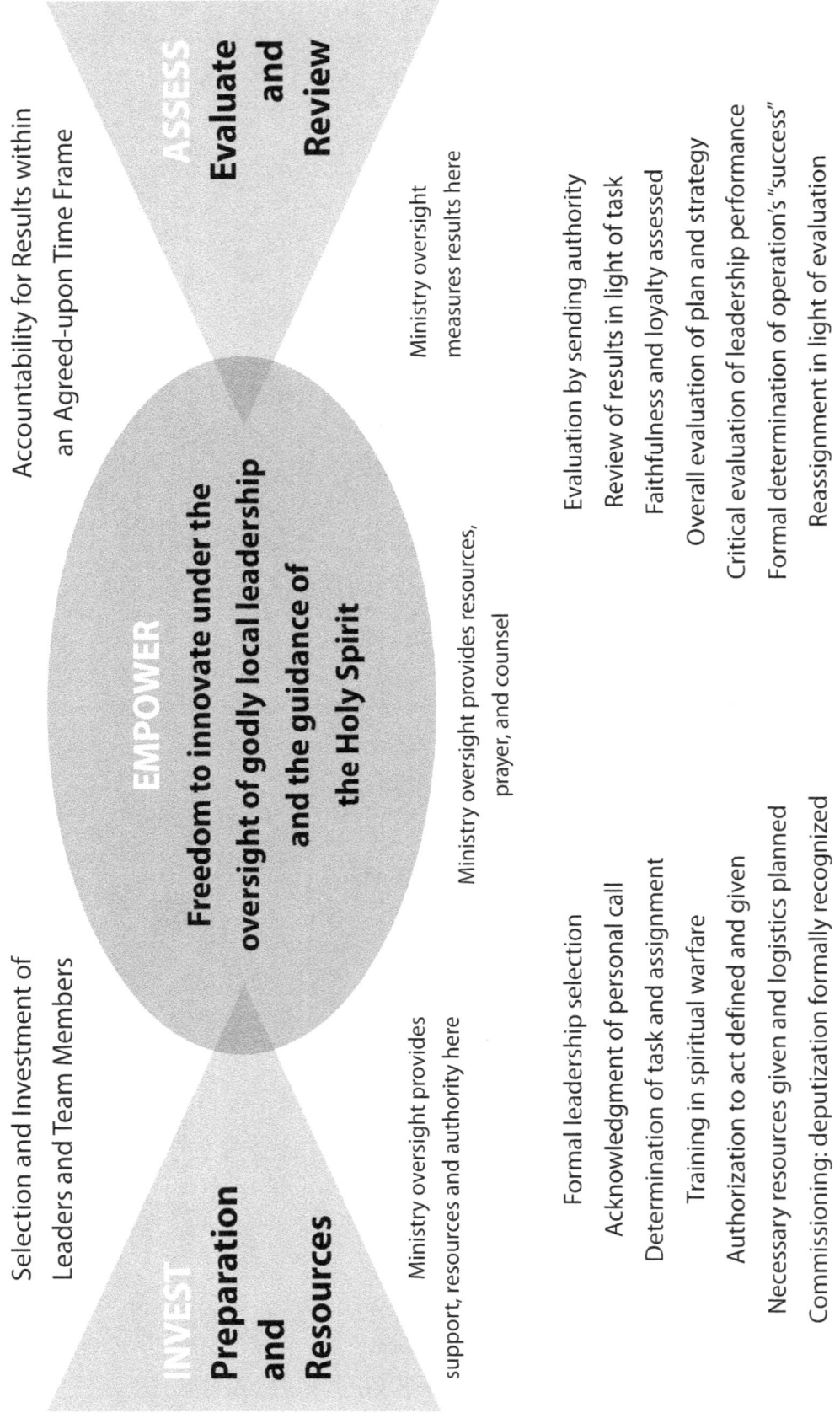

ASSESS

Evaluate and Review

Accountability for Results within an Agreed-upon Time Frame

Ministry oversight measures results here

Evaluation by sending authority
Review of results in light of task
Faithfulness and loyalty assessed
Overall evaluation of plan and strategy
Critical evaluation of leadership performance
Formal determination of operation's "success"
Reassignment in light of evaluation

EMPOWER

Freedom to innovate under the oversight of godly local leadership and the guidance of the Holy Spirit

Ministry oversight provides resources, prayer, and counsel

Selection and Investment of Leaders and Team Members

Ministry oversight provides support, resources and authority here

Formal leadership selection
Acknowledgment of personal call
Determination of task and assignment
Training in spiritual warfare
Authorization to act defined and given
Necessary resources given and logistics planned
Commissioning: deputization formally recognized

INVEST

Preparation and Resources

APPENDIX 8

Fit to Represent: Multiplying Disciples of the Kingdom of God

Rev. Dr. Don L. Davis

Luke 10.16 (ESV) - The one who hears you hears me, and the one who rejects you rejects me, and the one who rejects me rejects him who sent me.

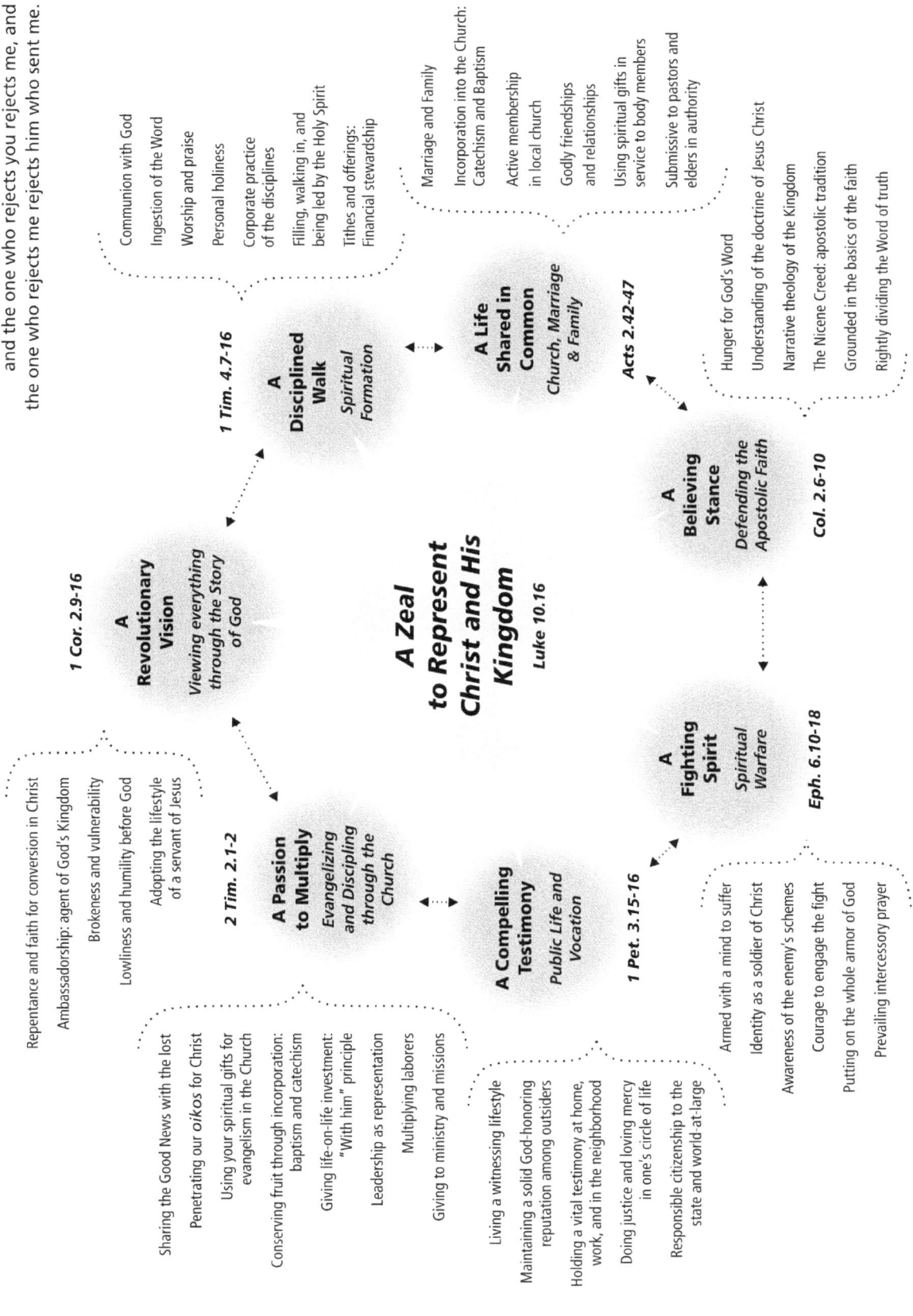

A Zeal to Represent Christ and His Kingdom
Luke 10.16

A Revolutionary Vision
Viewing everything through the Story of God
1 Cor. 2.9-16

- Repentance and faith for conversion in Christ
- Ambassadorship: agent of God's Kingdom
- Brokenness and vulnerability
- Lowliness and humility before God
- Adopting the lifestyle of a servant of Jesus

A Disciplined Walk
Spiritual Formation
1 Tim. 4.7-16

- Communion with God
- Ingestion of the Word
- Worship and praise
- Personal holiness
- Corporate practice of the disciplines
- Filling, walking in, and being led by the Holy Spirit
- Tithes and offerings: Financial stewardship

A Life Shared in Common
Church, Marriage & Family
Acts 2.42-47

- Marriage and Family
- Incorporation into the Church: Catechism and Baptism
- Active membership in local church
- Godly friendships and relationships
- Using spiritual gifts in service to body members
- Submissive to pastors and elders in authority

A Believing Stance
Defending the Apostolic Faith
Col. 2.6-10

- Hunger for God's Word
- Understanding of the doctrine of Jesus Christ
- Narrative theology of the Kingdom
- The Nicene Creed: apostolic tradition
- Grounded in the basics of the faith
- Rightly dividing the Word of truth

A Passion to Multiply
Evangelizing and Discipling through the Church
2 Tim. 2.1-2

- Sharing the Good News with the lost
- Penetrating our *oikos* for Christ
- Using your spiritual gifts for evangelism in the Church
- Conserving fruit through incorporation: baptism and catechism
- Giving life-on-life investment: "With him" principle
- Leadership as representation
- Multiplying laborers
- Giving to ministry and missions

A Compelling Testimony
Public Life and Vocation
1 Pet. 3.15-16

- Living a witnessing lifestyle
- Maintaining a solid God-honoring reputation among outsiders
- Holding a vital testimony at home, work, and in the neighborhood
- Doing justice and loving mercy in one's circle of life
- Responsible citizenship to the state and world-at-large

A Fighting Spirit
Spiritual Warfare
Eph. 6.10-18

- Armed with a mind to suffer
- Identity as a soldier of Christ
- Awareness of the enemy's schemes
- Courage to engage the fight
- Putting on the whole armor of God
- Prevailing intercessory prayer

APPENDIX 9

Responsibility Versus Resourcing in Representation

Rev. Dr. Don L. Davis

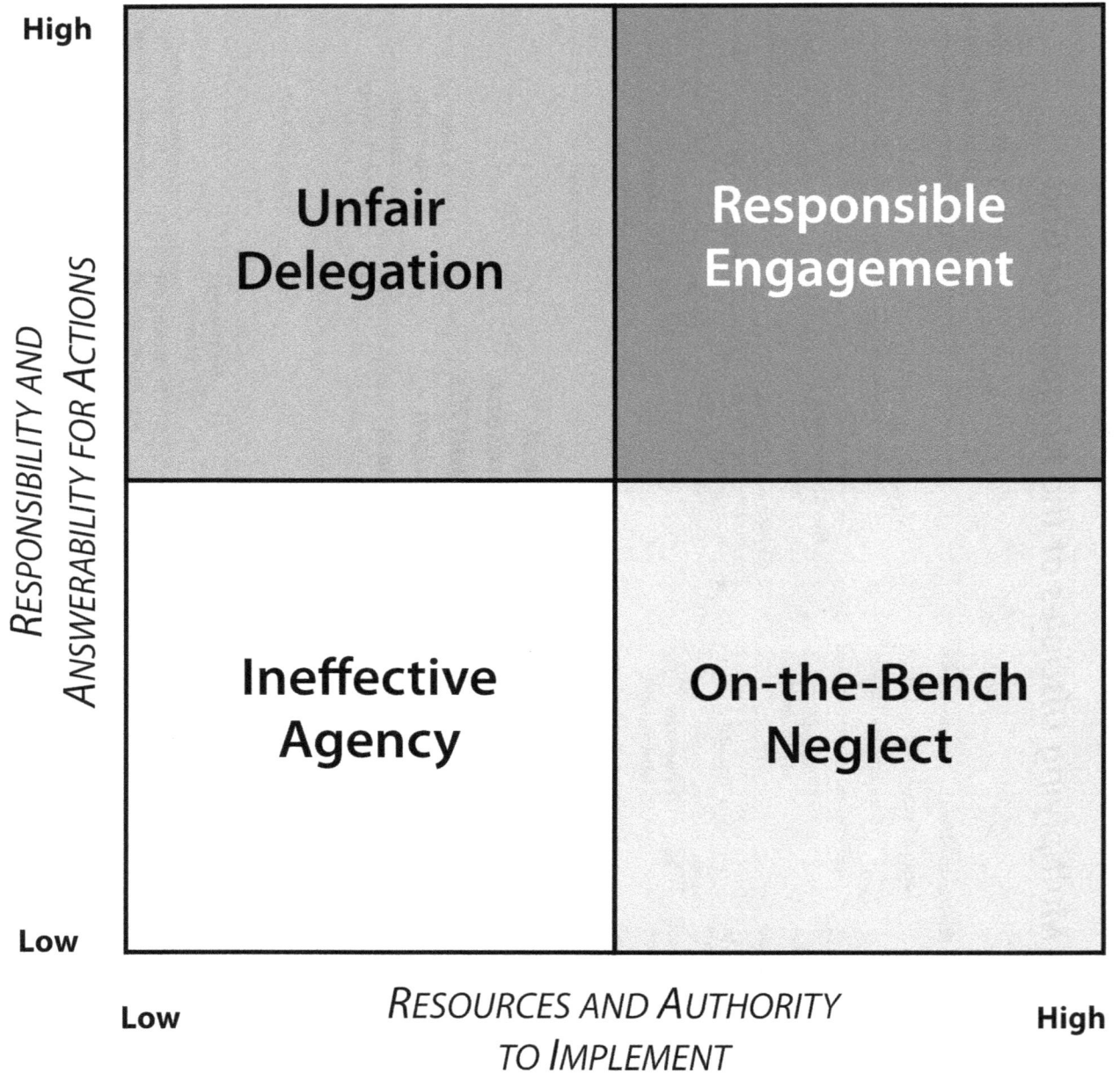

	Low ← RESOURCES AND AUTHORITY TO IMPLEMENT → High	
High ↑ RESPONSIBILITY AND ANSWERABILITY FOR ACTIONS	**Unfair Delegation**	**Responsible Engagement**
Low	**Ineffective Agency**	**On-the-Bench Neglect**

RESPONSIBILITY AND ANSWERABILITY FOR ACTIONS

High

Low

Low   RESOURCES AND AUTHORITY
TO IMPLEMENT   High

Becoming Like Your Teacher
Developing Effective Church Planting Apprenticeships

Preface

> He also told them a parable: "Can a blind man lead a blind man? Will they not both fall into a pit? A disciple is not above his teacher, but everyone when he is fully trained will be like his teacher."
>
> ~ Luke 6.39-40

Leadership is very much following somebody who presumes to know exactly where we need to go.

Jesus provides this simple definition of leadership to explain the necessity of every leader to be worthy of a follower-ship. Isn't it obvious that a person who cannot see, who is actually blind, should not be in the business of leading others around? Following such a person will inevitably not end well – "will they not both fall into a pit?" Jesus teaches that a disciple (a learner dedicated to follow the teaching and example of another) is not above his teacher, but, after the training process is fully complete, it is enough that the disciple "will be like his teacher." Here, Jesus gives a clear definition of discipleship: becoming like your teacher.

Such a simple formula should not be ignored. Training requires a teacher, someone worthy to be followed, someone whose experience, judgment, and understanding place them in a role to train and teach others. It also requires a disciple, someone who willingly and voluntarily submits themselves to the regimen, discipline, and training that a teacher provides. The end of the process is identification: after the disciple is fully trained, he will become just like his teacher. Real discipling, by this definition, is a form of apprenticeship.

An apprentice is a person who works for another to learn a trade or skill, historically, a learner who binds herself to a master craftsman in order to become a master herself. This idea of being bound to another to become like them is a fundamental way of learning all things, shown in the most natural and informal manner to the most skilled professional tradesmen. Perhaps the best way to learn a skill or trade is to find a person who is expert at it, and learn from the association. You watch them, accompany them, learn from them as they supervise you, allow

Becoming Like Your Teacher: Developing Effective Church Planting Apprenticeships, continued

yourself to be taught, corrected, and coached by them in order to become like them. This form of learning is simple, clean, efficient, and effective. All you need is a master and a student able and willing to pay the price to learn from the master.

We are convinced that for church planting, no method is as efficient and effective as apprenticeship. The best way to "apprehend" (to grasp the meaning of, to understand and perceive) a skill is to learn under someone who themselves have apprehended it first. To come under a leader in a field is the best way to learn the field. This is the standard for a number of trades: medicine, science, academics, construction, and music. The best way to understand something in that field is to learn it from someone well schooled, long experienced, and deeply trained in the field. This wisdom can be powerfully embraced in our church planting and pastoring contexts. When a disciple is fully trained, Jesus asserts, they will become just like their teacher.

While this does suggest that a bad teacher will train bad disciples, it also asserts that strong, clear teachers will equip strong clear disciples. At a time when we need scores of young, aggressive, and effective church planters, the call for apprenticeship programs and mentors must go out strong. We need churches, church plants, and outreach ministries to open their doors and their hearts to designing and hosting apprenticeship programs that will multiply the number of effective, emerging leaders as quickly as possible. No other form of leadership development is as clear, compelling, and compassionate as apprentice-ships; multiplying the number of worthy interns and candidates to learn the art and skill of church planting could revolutionize our impact in urban mission and outreach, and in the number of souls won to Christ.

This booklet is only meant to be a primer, a "tablespoon out of the pot" tidbit of the good wisdom and insights associated with church planting apprenticeships. If reading this tract makes the reader either more willing to prayerfully consider starting an apprenticeship program, or becoming an apprentice, its creation will be worth the effort. Join us in identifying a generation of worthy church planters who can be apprenticed to learn how to plant and prosper healthy communities of Christ in neighborhoods where he is not yet known and worshiped. Let us invest in an army of candidates ready to reproduce themselves for the sake of the Kingdom. Read this tract carefully. Start right away. The Spirit will lead you, and you will bear fruit, the kind that remains and multiplies.

Bob Engel, Newark, New Jersey
Don Davis, Wichita, Kansas
August 9, 2018

Becoming Like Your Teacher: Developing Effective Church Planting Apprenticeships, continued

Introduction

> War – Hard apprenticeship of Freedom.
>
> ~ Edward Everett Hale

With the incarnation and ministry of Jesus of Nazareth, the Messiah, the Kingdom of God has come! Christ Jesus has made a public spectacle of Satan, his minions, and all that the Kingdom of Darkness represents. He is God's Champion and Commander of his heavenly hosts. At the same time the Kingdom is yet to come. We live in the age of the Church who presses forward in the expansion and advancement of the Kingdom of God. As C. S. Lewis stated, "Enemy-occupied territory – that is what this world is. Christianity is the story of how the rightful king has landed, you might say landed in disguise, and is calling us to take part in a great campaign of sabotage."

You are following in the footsteps and calling of the first saboteurs, the Apostle Paul and Barnabas (Acts 11.25, 26, 30; 12.25; 13.1-3). Like them and the countless missionary saints after them, we all must enter into an apprentice phase until that time comes when the Spirit of the Lord, through the Elders, says, "Set apart for me Barnabas and Paul for the work to which I have called them." Whether you are hosting such a program or believe that God has called you to participate within one, you will need to trust the Lord to provide you with all you will require to fulfill your duty in Christ. We all must gladly submit to that full range of responsibilities as servants in the church for the purpose of being set apart by the Holy Spirit to engage in the Great Commission of our Lord Jesus. As his ambassador, you are called to evangelize, make disciples, raise up leaders and establish a new church in "enemy-occupied territory" for the glory of God.

Being a representative for Jesus with the task of planting an outpost of the Kingdom of God requires nothing less than a ready response to his call to ministry, sharing the life of Christ as his chosen vessel and servant. As the demon told the sons of Sceva, referring to authentic spiritual identity, "Jesus I know, and Paul I recognize" (Acts 19.15b). With the foundation of Christ confirmed in you and the mantle of his calling upon you, you can both offer or undergo rigorous and disciplined church planting training. If you are hosting an apprenticeship program, you can be God's chosen instrument to raise up laborers for Christ. If you are called as an apprentice, you can be equipped in order that you may become competent and fully assured to go and accomplish the task the Lord has given you.

Becoming Like Your Teacher: Developing Effective Church Planting Apprenticeships, continued

Code of Conduct: TUMI's Mission-Critical Perspectives

When you are deployed in enemy-occupied territory to establish a church (which literally is an outpost of the Kingdom of God), you will encounter spiritual opposition. Our spiritual combatant, the evil one, has gone before you and filled your target area with spiritual land mines and barriers designed to wound, kill, and destroy you and your team. His goal is to sabotage your efforts, rendering inoperative your work and the task you have been called and commissioned to accomplish. Our perspectives regarding our task and end are like metal detectors that give you a warning when you sweep over a potential mine. They are more than sufficient to help you side-step and eliminate these spiritual mines of destruction.

Now is the time, as a church planter apprentice, to know your "metal detector." Church planters and their team are involved in making hundreds of decisions every day. The decisions they make are built upon clearly articulated and held perspectives that shape your actions, and determine your strategies. Indeed, your perspectives help to direct you towards your specific purpose, that particular calling and task that the risen Lord has commissioned you to accomplish. This unique calling has been affirmed and recognized by Christ's Church and confirmed by his own Holy Spirit.

When walking through enemy-occupied territory, you will refer and reflect upon your perspectives in order to:

1. *Make decisions.* We make a deliberate choice to focus on what is important to us. Your perspectives shape your values, which when affirmed and shared, mobilizes your team into a cohesive squad.

2. *Stand strong.* When the enemy attacks your mind with his deceptive lies about who you are in Christ, your biblically informed perspectives will empower you to stand strong. Your worth is built on who God declares you to be in Christ. Who you are is more important than what you do.

3. *Give focus.* When the task becomes too much, unclear, or a formidable struggle, your renewed perspectives provide focus, direction, motivation to not shrink back but to believe and press onward.

Becoming Like Your Teacher: Developing Effective Church Planting Apprenticeships, continued

TUMI's Mission-Critical Perspectives

The Calling of God

And we know that for those who love God all things work together for good, for those who are called according to his purpose.

~ Romans 8.28

We do all we do fully assured that God is at this very moment calling, gifting, and anointing men and women in the city to represent his interests there, and are convinced that these chosen city leaders will be the vessels through whom he advances his Kingdom.

The Kingdom of God

But seek first the kingdom of God and his righteousness, and all these things will be added to you.

~ Matthew 6.33

We are burdened to see the freedom, wholeness, and justice of the Kingdom of God embodied, celebrated, and proclaimed in church communities who show visibly what the "Rule of God" looks like when it is embraced by people who acknowledge Christ's lordship.

The Centrality of the Church

. . . if I delay, you may know how one ought to behave in the household of God, which is the church of the living God, a pillar and buttress of the truth.

~ 1 Timothy 3.15

We hold deeply the conviction that effective ministry takes place in the Body of Christ, the agent of the Kingdom, where we facilitate the multiplication of healthy, reproducing urban churches, especially among the poor.

Becoming Like Your Teacher: Developing Effective Church Planting Apprenticeships, continued

The Power of Community

Now you are the body of Christ and individually members of it.

~ 1 Corinthians 12.27

We share a passion to employ innovative distance education programming to create and outfit a network of training centers in urban areas that provide excellent, affordable, and spiritually dynamic ministry education that is sensitive to urban culture.

God's Election of the Humble

Listen, my beloved brothers, has not God chosen those who are poor in the world to be rich in faith and heirs of the kingdom, which he has promised to those who love him?

~ James 2.5

We possess a certitude that God has chosen those who are poor in the eyes of this world to be rich in faith and to inherit the Kingdom which he promised to those who love him (James 2.5).

The Standard of Excellence

So, whether you eat or drink, or whatever you do, do all to the glory of God.

~ 1 Corinthians 10.31

We are held by the consuming belief that all effective, credible leadership development demands the requisite formality and rigor of disciplined excellence, with a flat refusal to be remedial or second-class.

The Explosiveness of Multiplication

. . . and what you have heard from me in the presence of many witnesses entrust to faithful men, who will be able to teach others also.

~ 2 Timothy 2.2

We are zealous to facilitate and empower urban church planting movements that share a common spirituality, express freedom in cultural expression, and strategically combine their resources to reach and transform the cities of America and the world.

Call of Duty: Church Planter Apprenticeship

God has created a system in the church whereby we can equip emerging leaders to accomplish his will under the tutelage of mature mentors and leaders. Apprenticeships are pre-defined terms of service and learning sponsored in the context of a supportive church/ministry, overseen by capable supervision which is designed to equip the apprentice in church planting among the poor.

"Pre-defined terms of service and learning." Apprenticeships should be limited to a specific term of service, with specific rules and guidelines for its length and work. We strongly suggest that you create a written contract of service that spells out precisely the bounds, privileges, and responsibilities of the apprenticeship, including its length, any remuneration offered, terms of service, and all other matters related to the apprentice's work and duties.

". . . in the context of a supportive church/ministry." Apprenticeships should be connected to a particular church or ministry which has formally agreed to oversee the apprentice, providing specific training and exposure to church planting among the poor.

". . . overseen by capable supervision." Apprenticeship's should be connected to specific mentors, supervisors, or leaders who supervise and oversee the apprentice's training, assignments and work. Apprentices should report to these supervisors who equip, encourage, and offer regular feedback as to the apprentice's progress or areas of growth needed to be worked on.

". . . which is designed to equip the apprentice in church planting among the poor." Apprenticeships are targeted to equip the individual to plant a church among the poor. Apprenticeships are not "special" in the sense of creating some unique and unrelated role for the apprentice. Rather, the best apprenticeship programs are connected specifically to training the apprentice to gain expertise and exposure for the task of planting a church that the church/ministry currently embraces, supports, and enhances the goals and priorities of that church/ministry.

Training interns in a wisely-supervised apprenticeship program is an effective means to multiply spiritual laborers for the harvest, and to equip servant-leaders for effective ministry in the church!

The Battle Plan: Confirm and Equip

From the start, we should assume that ministry candidates will come to us at various levels of maturity and development, i.e., in their overall understanding of Scripture, living a Christ-centered life and missions. Each indigenous urban church planter must already possess the requisite maturity and experience to be considered a worthy candidate in an apprenticeship program.

Indeed, a solid apprenticeship requires great care and focus done well in advance of the learning experience to guarantee its success. In other words, ministry supervisors must take the time to map out a measurable and feasible apprentice plan and overall schedule. In addition, time must be given to determine the substance of the apprenticeship, including assignments, field work, time for study and critical reflection, and whatever financial resources and staff support the apprenticeship program will provide. Until these critical features have been carefully considered and decided, no church plant apprenticeship program should be commenced!

It is foundational that any individual who wants to enlist into an Apprentice Program, must have the blessing and confirmation of his/her leaders. It is the church leadership who must discern and confirm the individuals calling and gifting. Great care and focus must be decided well in advance of the apprenticeship to guarantee its success. The Apostle Paul, though called and gifted by the Lord Jesus himself, still submitted himself to the leadership of the local church in Antioch.

The leadership of a local church has the final say-so for those seeking confirmation to serve in a church planter apprenticeship program. Online programs, written tests, or the individual's "feelings" are all subservient to the leadership in which the prospective apprentice submits and honors. Outside aids can be a supplement for leadership as they pray and seek the Spirit's leading and confirmation. One such aid is TUMI's* Evangel Church Planter's Assessment. This excellent tool can assist church leadership in their vetting process.

---

* The Urban Ministry Institute (TUMI), the national training arm for World Impact, equips leadership for the urban church, especially among the poor, in order to advance the Kingdom of God. We focus our investment on those called to evangelize, disciple, plant, and pastor churches in unreached urban neighborhoods. Our single passion and desire is to identify, empower, and release laborers who can both display and declare God's kingdom reign among their neighbors, where they live. Learn more by going to: *www.tumi.org*.

*Becoming Like Your Teacher:
Developing Effective Church
Planting Apprenticeships,*
continued

There are four areas of church planter training that are foundational to Designing your Church Planter Apprenticeship Program. These are:

1. *Leadership Development.* "Survival of the fittest is not the same as survival of the best. Leaving leadership development up to chance is foolish" (Morgan McCall). Designing your leadership development track requires prayer and intentionality. One size does not fit all. Leaders are made, not born. You must know your apprentice and what they need to make them into a leader.

   For example, Dr. Davis's (Executive Director, The Urban Ministry Institute) *Get Your Pretense On!* outlines a biblical and doctrinal perspective designed to help any disciple of Christ know what it means to act worthy of your true, redeemed status and position, and to make a difference in the roles where Jesus has placed you. Two of the chapters, "There's Plenty Good Room: The Centrality of the Church in God's Kingdom Advance", and "The *Oikos* Factor: Being Used of God to Change Your World" are excellent readings for dialogue and discussion in your church planter apprentice regimen. The concepts in this book will prove invaluable for your apprentice in their leadership development.

2. *Biblical and Theological Training.* *"As we have said before, so now I say again: If anyone is preaching to you a gospel contrary to the one you received, let him be accursed"* (Gal. 1.9).

   From the beginning of history, the enemy has sought to twist and malign God's Word. A half-truth is always a full lie. The Church's history is filled with women and men who sacrificed their lives for the defense of the Church's confession, what it has "believed everywhere, always and by all." A solid apprenticeship program respects this; a good one always has a quality biblical and theological training component.

   Thousands of students and hundreds of satellites use The Urban Ministry Institute's *Capstone Curriculum* around the world. This resource, as well as hundreds of other curriculum resources, are available to you as you design your own, unique and personalized apprenticeship program to hone in on your apprentice's biblical and theological areas of growth.

3. *Church Planting Experience* (Field Work/Boots on the Ground). *"And he appointed twelve (whom he also named apostles) so that they might be with him and he might send them out to preach"* (Mark 3.14).

Becoming Like Your Teacher: Developing Effective Church Planting Apprenticeships, continued

An apprenticeship is not just about books to read and assignments to be completed. The best apprenticeships occur when the pastor and other leaders personally invest into the life of the apprentice. Jesus prayed and called twelve apostles to *"be with him."* He spent time with them, asked them questions, invited them to participate with him in ministry, and eventually sent them out to make disciples of all nations. In effective discipleship, there is simply no substitute for individualized, personal, and relational investment.

4. *Spiritual Growth.* "Therefore let us leave the elementary doctrine of Christ and go on to maturity, not laying again a foundation of repentance from dead works and of faith toward God" (Heb. 6.1).

God expects each of his children to mature in Christ, to develop into full adults in him. Like our own children, such maturity will not happen overnight nor by chance. Good loving parental care is intentional. Such care provides input for the purpose of maturity, and it necessarily implements the refining responsibilities along each of life's growth stages. Just like a developing child, in similar fashion, an apprentice needs the necessary spiritual formation to grow into a mature disciple. That maturity is essential for each one who feels called to serve the Commander of the Lords Army in every situation.

One of the great problems in our contemporary spiritual formation is the sheer number of diverse, non-integrated ideas, resources, and themes in the ongoing lives of Christian communities today. This patchwork of disconnected approaches and ideas rubs against our natural disposition to focus on an idea, one big, integrated idea for an extended period. For those of us who see Christ Jesus as the source and center of the Christian experience, this recurring focus on dozens of disconnected ideas sabotages effective, biblical spiritual formation.

It is our conviction that God can deepen us in a single spiritual concept for an entire year, with focused disciplined study and reflection for most of it. The Urban Ministry Institute's *Sacred Roots Annual* centers the apprentice's life around a shared theme for the entire journey of the Church Year. The apprentice can effectively then become focused on a single spiritual theme for the entire year rather than being scattered around a multitude of themes. Such a focus can enable your church family and community to center itself on a Christ-centered focus, one that allows you to grow deeper around a significant biblical theme that the Spirit wishes you to know, feel, and experience together.

These are just a few examples of the many tools that are available to you from the TUMI church planting arsenal. You design your apprenticeship program to fit your vision and goals. TUMI deliberately seeks to strengthen your hand as you design and run your own program, for the purposes and ends that you have set for it. From a spiritual perspective, TUMI adopts the old Home Depot slogan, "You can do it! We can help."

Field Ready: Six Fitness Marks before Commissioning

The Armed Services Vocational Aptitude Battery (ASVAB) is a multiple-choice test, administered by the United States Military Entrance Processing Command, used to determine qualification for enlistment in the United States Armed Forces. To enter into the Special Forces, individuals have to reach the highest marks on the ASVAB tests. If these predetermined marks are not attained, the individual doesn't move into the Special Forces. They move into a different roll within the Military.

Scriptures mandate and give examples to, "not be too quick on the laying of hands." If not taken seriously, great harm can come upon the individual and the Community. We are in a spiritual war and the enemy is out to kill, steal, and destroy. Everyone is called to engage and participate in God's kingdom movement but not everyone has the same calling. The calling to evangelize, make disciples and establish a new church is not a calling for everyone.

Before commissioning individuals to church plant, there are six marks that must clearly be a part of the church planter. A quality apprenticeship program will strengthen each of these marks so that in partnership with the Holy Spirit, leadership can say, "Now set apart for me." These marks are:

1. *Master the art and discipline of being a worthy leader.* The apprentice must be able to feed themselves spiritually through a variety of spiritual disciplines (1 Tim. 4.7-8). The task of church planting requires, demands, one who is sensitive to the leading of the Holy Spirit and is quick to respond in obedience (Acts 16.6-10).

2. *Engage in personal evangelism and spiritual warfare.* The apprentice must know how to engage in evangelism that leads the hearer to a point of response. Engaging spiritual warfare through prayer will be foundational (Rom. 1.16; Eph. 6.18).

3. *Follow up new Christians and disciple them in the spiritual disciplines.* The apprentice must know how to lead a convert to be a disciple of

Jesus. He/she has to be skilled in doing this through formal curriculum and life relationships (Matt. 28.19-20).

4. ***Do the work of a pastor, shepherding others and fulfilling pastoral responsibilities.*** The apprentice must have the necessary gifts, character, and skills to "shepherd the flock."

5. ***Understand and be committed to the principles of spiritual reproduction and church planting movements.*** There must be clear observation and communication from the Apprentice that, "none should perish." The apprentice must understand the vastness of the harvest field and the importance of reproduction and multiplying themselves to create church planting movements (2 Tim. 2.2; 1 Thess. 1.8).

6. ***Possess a strategic vision for contributing to the Great Commission, and a practical plan to implement it.*** The apprentice must have a vision from the Lord that burns within them and a plan to unleash this Spirit-given vision. To assist in helping birth the vision through a Spirit driven strategic process we recommend enlisting into the *Evangel School of Urban Church Planting.* (Visit *www.tumi.org* for more details.)

Checklist: All Systems Are Go!

We are held by the consuming belief that all effective, credible leadership development demands the requisite formality and rigor of disciplined excellence, with a flat refusal to be remedial or second-class. To ensure that quality is maintained, your program should commit to cover all the major areas of both designing and managing an effective apprenticeship program. All elements of the program must be done excellently, in proper order, and professionally carried out for the benefit of both the church and the apprentice. This following checklist will assist you in developing an excellent apprentice program for the glory of God and the furtherance of his Kingdom.

YOUR APPRENTICESHIP PROGRAM CHECKLIST

Determine the Area Your Apprenticeships Will Be Offered (Choose all that apply)

❑ Church Planter

❑ Pastoral Care

❑ Worship/Music

❑ Children and Youth Ministry

❏ Teacher

❏ Counselor

Sketch the General Shape and Scope of Your Proposed Apprenticeship

❏ Think through the details of your Battle Plan (see pages 48-51).

❏ Define precisely the purpose of this apprenticeship. *State concisely why you are hosting it.*

❏ What ministry areas will be impacted by this apprenticeship? *Where will it occur?*

❏ Qualifications (age, education, character). *What demands do you need for candidates to meet?*

❏ When/Duration. *How long do you envision the apprenticeship to last?*

❏ Time Commitment. *How much time will you allot to the apprenticeship investment per week?*

❏ Remuneration. *How much money/support do you intend to provide to the apprentice?*

❏ Housing. *If housing is a portion of your support, where will it be, and what will it involve?*

Create and Circulate Your Candidate Application Form

❏ Contact Information. *Obtain all personal contact information needed for the candidate including name, address, phone, e-mail, etc.*

❏ Testimony (paragraph). *Have the candidate list their personal story of their journey to Jesus, their personal walk and faith, and their ongoing life in Christ today.*

❏ Goals of the Apprenticeship. *The candidate should list their goals and objectives (their expectations) for the apprenticeship.*

❏ Legal record (if any). *Have the candidate list any history they may have had with law enforcement, any pending situations, or any convictions as it relates to the law and the state.*

❏ Doctrinal Response Questions. *Have the candidate respond to your statement of faith, listing their commitment to represent it, and willingness to abide by its strictures.*

❏ Statement of Faith Agreement. *Have the candidate sign your statement of faith.*

❏ Recommendation. *Ensure lead pastor and relevant staff accept the candidate's choice.*

Map Out Carefully How You Will Deal with Issues and Rough Edges (Rules of Engagement)

❏ Think through scenarios and map out how you will deal with tough situations (*e.g., insubordination, ineffective work, moral compromise, conflict management*).

❏ Detail the accountability structure you will have for the apprenticeship (*e.g., weekly review meetings covering both spiritual growth and ministerial responsibility*).

❏ Communicate clearly the supervisory structure (*e.g., what are they responsible for, to who will they report, how often, what form [whether face-to-face, written, both?]*).

❏ Provide instruction in how to handle emergency situations during the apprenticeship (*e.g., who to contact, things to be aware of, procedures for at-risk circumstances*).

Finalize and Implement Your Internship/Apprenticeship Program

❏ Formally interview, consider, and offer the apprenticeship opportunity to your selected candidate.

❏ Announce your selection to the staff and congregation.

❏ Prepare for the apprenticeship's launch date, and arrange all necessary details to implement it.

❏ Implement the Apprenticeship program, adapting your schedule and content as you go.

❏ Once completed, recognize the intern, formally celebrating their accomplishment and contribution.

❏ Counsel the apprentice on what the next steps should be not that the apprenticeship has been completed.

Let's Take This City for God

From the time of Pentecost, the apostolic-missionary movement has unfurled through the centuries to herald the Good News of redemption to the lost. That Good News is clear: when unbelievers respond to the Gospel in believing faith and confession, they are free from the penalty of sin, transferred into Christ's Kingdom of righteousness, joy and peace. Since the time of the apostles, God has looked for select men and women who are filled with his Spirit to courageously go and make disciples of all the nations. Today, the "nations" (people groups) of the world have migrated to our inner cities. Quite literally, if we take our cities for God through the proclamation of the Gospel and making disciples of the faithful, we can reach the nations of the world and not even cross an ocean! The peoples of the world have come to our doorstep; all we need is the resolve to win them, gather them into outposts of the Kingdom, and see them deployed to their kin folk and neighbors as ambassadors of Jesus Christ.

Let us always be aware that in this expansion of God's kingdom authority in the earth we face a ruthless and cunning enemy, who is determined to undermine all that we do as we seek to obey our Lord. Of course, the Church Militant has been given her mission orders from her Lord. Our King Jesus, triumphant and risen, is undeterred by the enemy's opposition. Even in the face of what appears to be insurmountable odds, he has given this specific charge to his church:

> God authorized and commanded me to commission you: Go out and train everyone you meet, far and near, in this way of life, marking them by baptism in the threefold name: Father, Son, and Holy Spirit. Then instruct them in the practice of all I have commanded you. I'll be with you as you do this, day after day after day, right up to the end of the age.
>
> ~ Matthew 28.19-20, *The Message*

In light of our Lord's command, then, this is the time to experiment, to be courageous. J. Oswald Sanders has said, "A great deal more failure is the result of an excess of caution than of bold experimentation with new ideas. The frontiers of the Kingdom of God were never advanced by men and women of caution." Too much is at stake for us to be "men and women of caution." We need more church planters, more folk called by God with apostolic gifting willing to go and make disciples of Jesus among the lost. How do we obtain them? We apprentice a new generation, ready and willing to respond!

We should remember always that the concept of apprenticeship is not a new idea. It continues to undergird the preparation of excellence in a number of fields (e.g., medicine, construction, academics), although it often times seems ignored or absent in our churches. The Evangel movement calls on the urban church to make alive this ancient way of raising up leaders once again.

Above all other things, we must embrace the Lord's command afresh. Let us not be the first Church era that fails and falters in our obedience to the commission of the Captain of the Lord's Army. Rather, may we together become that generation of Christ followers who surrender everything to take our cities for God. Let us give our all to equip thousands upon thousands of apprentices whom the Spirit will deploy as some of the finest, most dedicated cadres of church planters that the modern missionary venture has ever witnessed. And, our heartfelt prayer is this: let this miracle happen among the poorest of the poor, the least of these, in the toughest, most unreached communities on the earth.

"So let it be written! So let it be done!"

Steps to Equipping Others

Rev. Dr. Don L. Davis

Step One

You become a Master at it, striving toward mastery by practicing it with regularity, excellence, and enjoyment. You must learn to do it, and do it excellently. While you need not be perfect, you should be able to do it, be doing it regularly, and growing in your practice of it. This is the most fundamental principle of all mentoring and discipling. You cannot teach what you do not know or cannot do, and when your Apprentice is fully trained, they will become like you (Luke 6.40).

Step Two

*You **select an Apprentice** who also desires to develop mastery of the thing, one who is teachable, faithful, and available.* Jesus called the Twelve to be with him, and to send them out to preach (Mark 3.14). His relationship was clear, neither vague nor coerced. The roles and responsibilities of the relationship must be carefully outlined, clearly discussed, and openly agreed upon.

Step Three

*You instruct and model the task **in the presence of and accompanied by** your Apprentice.* He/she comes alongside you to listen, observe, and watch. You do it with regularity and excellence, and your Apprentice comes along "for the ride," who is brought along to see how it is done. A picture is worth a thousand words. This sort of non-pressure participant observation is critical to in-depth training (2 Tim. 2.2; Phil. 4.9).

Step Four

*You do the task and **practice the thing together**.* Having modeled the act for your Apprentice in many ways and at many times, you now invite them to cooperate with you by becoming a partner-in-training, working together on the task. The goal is to do the task together, taking mutual responsibility. You coordinate your efforts, working together in harmony to accomplish the thing.

Step Five

*Your Apprentice does the task on their own, **in the presence of and accompanied by you**.* You provide opportunity to your Apprentice to practice the thing in your presence while you watch and listen. You make yourself available to help, but offer it in the background; you provide counsel, input, and guidance as they request it, but they do the task. Afterwards, you evaluate and clarify anything you may have observed as you accompanied your Apprentice (2 Cor. 11.1).

Step Six

*Your Apprentice does the thing solo, practicing it regularly, automatically, and excellently **until mastery of the thing is gained**.* After your Apprentice has done the task under your supervision excellently, he/she is ready to be released to make the thing his/her own by habituating the act in his/her own life. You are a co-doer with your Apprentice; both of you are doing the task without coercion or aid from the other. The goal is familiarity and skillfulness in the task (Heb. 5.11-15).

Step Seven

*Your Apprentice **becomes a Mentor of others**, selecting other faithful Apprentices to equip and train.* The training process bears fruit when the Apprentice, having mastered the thing you have equipped him/her to do, becomes a trainer of others. This is the heart of the discipling and training process (Heb. 5.11-14; 2 Tim. 2.2).

Appendix 12

From Seeker to Sensei:
Developing Effective Movement Apprenticeships

Rev. Dr. Don L. Davis

> A disciple is not above his teacher, but everyone when he is fully trained will be like his teacher.
>
> ~ Jesus, Luke 6.40 (ESV)
>
> *Seeker*: a person or thing that seeks
>
> ~ dictionary.com
> *https://www.dictionary.com/browse/seeker?s=t*
>
> *Sensei*: (can be pronounced "Sensai" as well), Sinsang, Sonsaeng, Seonsaeng or Xiansheng is an honorific term shared in Chinese honorifics and Japanese honorifics that is translated as "person born before another" or "one who comes before.
>
> ~ Wikipedia
> *https://en.wikipedia.org/wiki/Sensei*

I. **The *Paradigm* of Apprenticeships: Movements, Leaders, and Apprenticeships**

   A. The Golden Strand: How do movements start, grow, and thrive?

      1. *Strand one:* The role of the founder: Moses

      2. *Strand two:* The synergy of the "first followers": Joshua

      3. *Strand three:* The strength of young apprentices in a tradition: Jehu, Gideon, Samson, Samuel

      4. The power of tradition: not a dirty word

         a. *Paradosis*: the handing down to another the invaluable deposit

         b. A mixture of content and loyalty

         c. *Traditioned innovation* (Dr. Alvin Sanders): building on the legacy given, engaging on the situation encountered

B. Why apprenticeships work among movements among the poor

1. They are *organic*: receiving protection, care, and training from another.

2. They are *affordable*: they require presence not funds.

3. They are *transparent*: you learn on the job in the presence of a valid leader.

4. They are *reliable*: authority is given after verified loyalty and service.

5. They are *reproducible*: once a system of apprenticeship is begun, it can be replicated indefinitely.

C. The biblical blueprint of a worthy apprenticeship

1. The call of *God*: a publicly acknowledged and confirmed call

2. The character of *Christ*: proven character in the midst of lived life

3. The charisma of the *Holy Spirit*: anointing and gifting in the Church

4. The connection to the *Church community*: compelling testimony within and among the people of the body

II. The *Process* of Apprenticeships: From Seeker to Sensei (*Steps to Equipping Others*)

A. Join the movement and commit to represent its identity, purpose, and mission.

B. Distinguish yourself in the movement as a champion of faithfulness of service.

C. Receive apprentices for future representation and authority in the movement.

D. Instruct and model movement representation task in the presence of and accompanied by the apprentices.

*From Seeker to Sensei:
Developing Effective
Movement Apprenticeships,*
continued

E. Co-labor in movement representation as colleagues and comrades together.

F. Give the apprentice solo assignments, with you only accompanying as support.

G. Assign the apprentice formal leadership status, i.e., to take on their own apprenticeships as agent of the movement.

III. The *Principle* of Apprenticeship: Leadership as Representation (*The Role of Formal Proxy: Leadership as Representation*)

A. Apostles, evangelists, prophets, and ambassadors: representatives of another

B. Jesus as the perfect pattern of the representative of God

C. The dynamics of representation

1. The *Commissioning*: formal selection and call

2. The *Equipping*: appropriate training and investment

3. The *Entrustment*: endowed with the authority and power to act on behalf of the movement

4. The *Mission*: faithful execution of the task

5. The *Reckoning*: assessment and evaluation of the results attained

6. The *Reward*: recognition and reward based on the faithful service and results attained

(See appendix *Understanding Leadership as Representation*)

IV. The *Problems* of Apprenticeships: The Rough Edges of Apprenticeship

A. *Movement creep*: Unclear as to what the movement is, stands for, or seeks to do

B. *Secret society*: No discernible path to join or align with our movement

C. *Unspoken pathways*: Neglect of specific ways movement folk can engage and represent the movement, whatever the level

D. *Phony channels of opportunity*: tolerating unhealthy folk or promoting folk with unproven track records among us

E. *No recognition or promotion*: failing to reward loyalty and service

V. The *Practice* of Apprenticeships: Take-aways for a New Vision

A. Clarify your movement play-book: Who, what, why, how . . .

B. Make the invitation: boldly, clearly, and often.

C. Ask God for insight into your choice of the next generation of leaders.

D. Offer specific roles, assignments for the most loyal "first followers."

E. Develop a workable, modest apprenticeship program, focused on investment.

F. Provide both oversight, provision, and answerability throughout the entire period.

G. Certify your apprentices: be ready to delegate the assignments and authority once the program is successfully completed.

Closing quotes from Sensei Mr. Miyagi

"Either you karate do 'yes' or karate do 'no.' You karate do 'guess so,' (get squished) just like grape."

The point: Once you commit to an enterprise, do it with your full heart and effort. Or not, and pay the price.

"Never trust a spiritual leader who cannot dance."

The point: Every true leader has to be flexible, adaptable, and able to enjoy themselves in the process. Correction and celebration!

APPENDIX 13

A Sociology of Urban Leadership Development
A Tool for Assessment and Training
Rev. Dr. Don L. Davis

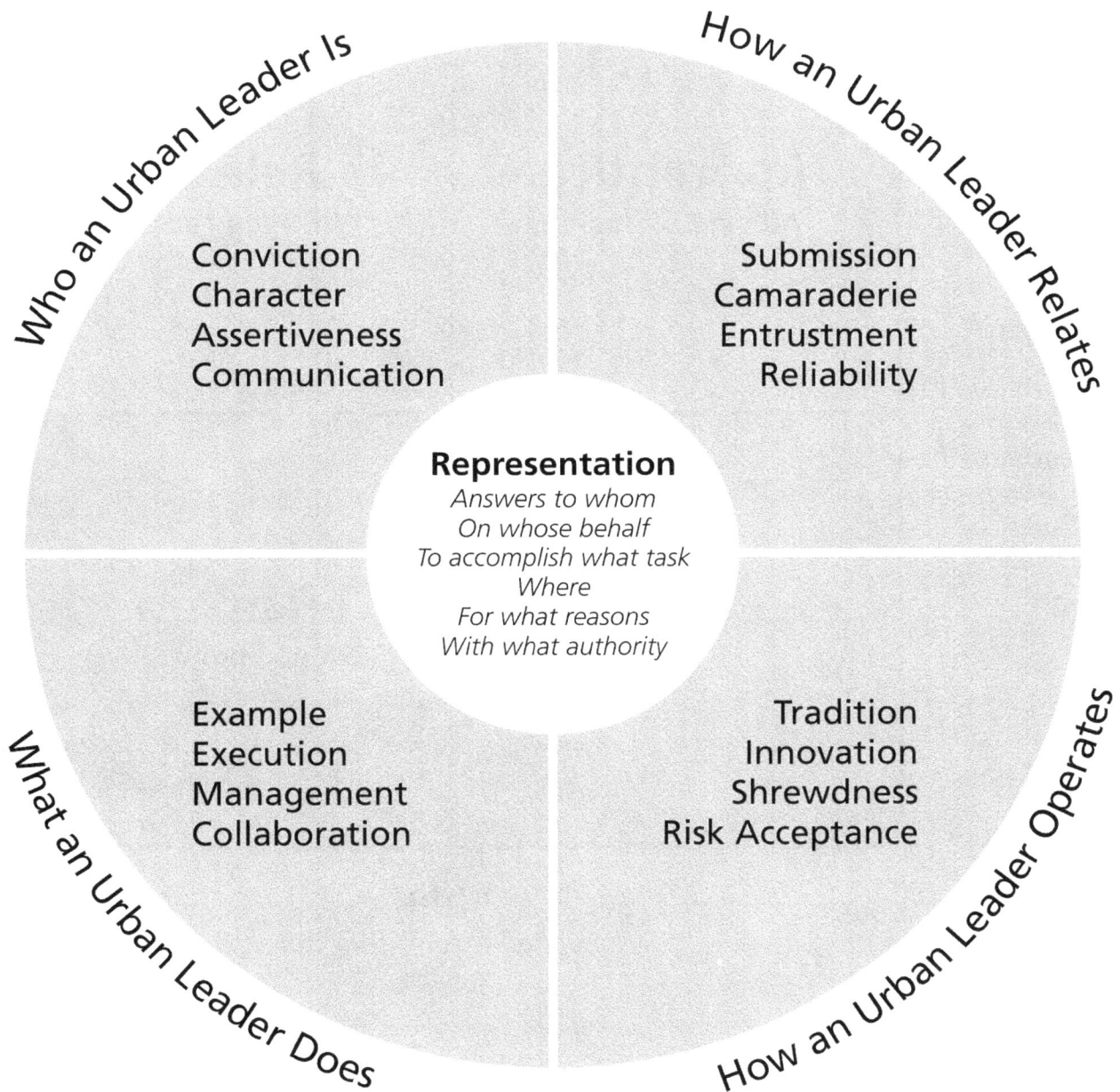

Who an Urban Leader Is

How an Urban Leader Relates

What an Urban Leader Does

How an Urban Leader Operates

Conviction
Character
Assertiveness
Communication

Submission
Camaraderie
Entrustment
Reliability

Representation
Answers to whom
On whose behalf
To accomplish what task
Where
For what reasons
With what authority

Example
Execution
Management
Collaboration

Tradition
Innovation
Shrewdness
Risk Acceptance

APPENDIX 14
Retooling for Maximum Contribution to Fulfill Our Vision
Rev. Dr. Don L. Davis

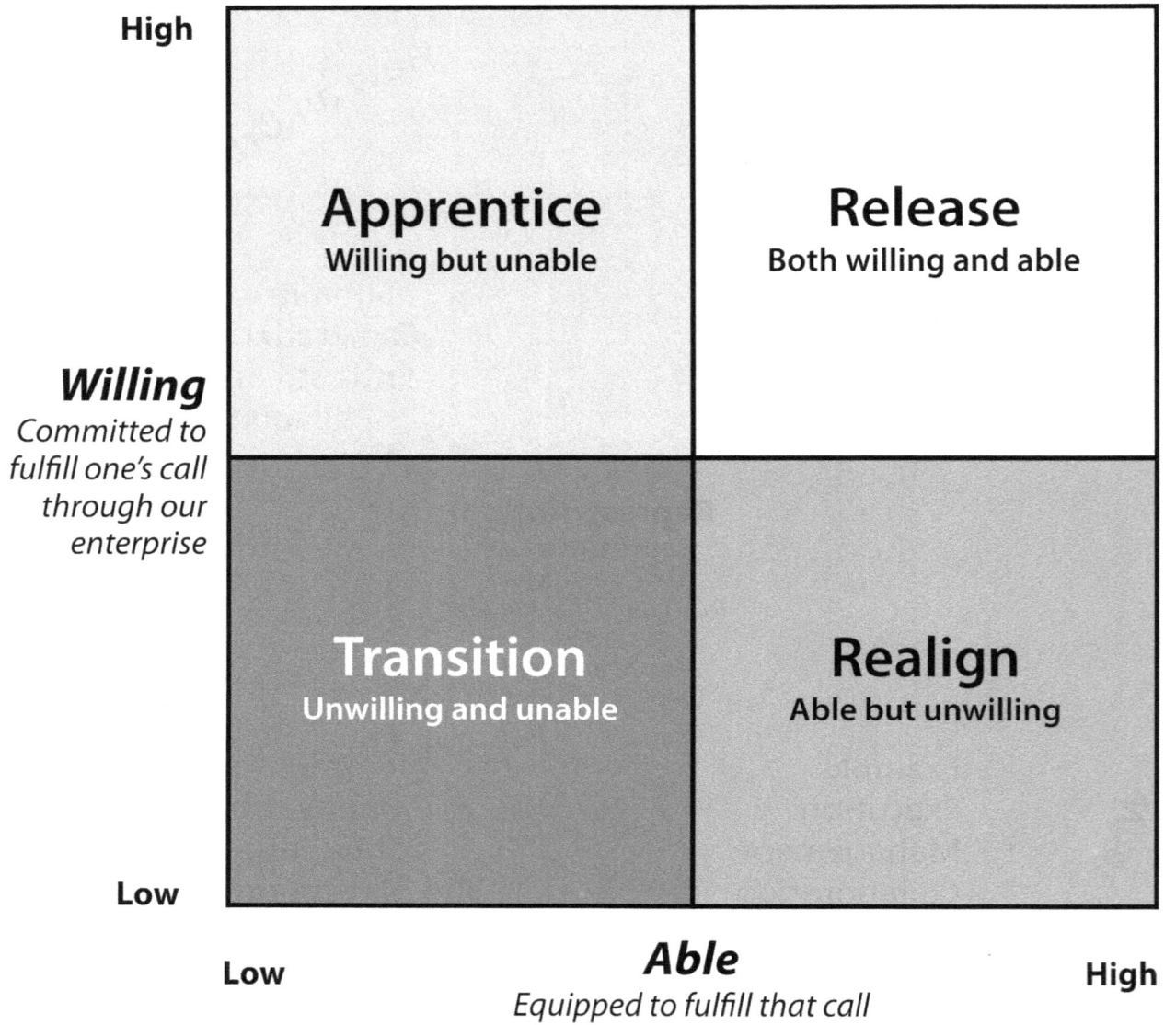

High

Apprentice Willing but unable	**Release** Both willing and able
Transition Unwilling and unable	**Realign** Able but unwilling

Willing
Committed to fulfill one's call through our enterprise

Low

Low   ***Able***   **High**
Equipped to fulfill that call

APPENDIX 15

The Story of God: Our Sacred Roots

Rev. Dr. Don L. Davis

The Alpha and the Omega	Christus Victor	Come, Holy Spirit	Your Word Is Truth	The Great Confession	His Life in Us	Living in the Way	Reborn to Serve
The LORD God is the source, sustainer, and end of all things in the heavens and earth. All things were formed and exist by his will and for his eternal glory, the triune God, Father, Son, and Holy Spirit. Rom. 11.36.							
THE TRIUNE GOD'S UNFOLDING DRAMA — God's Self-Revelation in Creation, Israel, and Christ				THE CHURCH'S PARTICIPATION IN GOD'S UNFOLDING DRAMA — Fidelity to the Apostolic Witness to Christ and His Kingdom			
The Objective Foundation: The Sovereign Love of God — God's Narration of His Saving Work in Christ				The Subjective Practice: Salvation by Grace through Faith — The Redeemed's Joyous Response to God's Saving Work in Christ			
The Author of the Story	*The Champion of the Story*	*The Interpreter of the Story*	*The Testimony of the Story*	*The People of the Story*	*Re-enactment of the Story*	*Embodiment of the Story*	*Continuation of the Story*
The Father as Director	Jesus as Lead Actor	The Spirit as Narrator	Scripture as Script	As Saints, Confessors	As Worshipers, Ministers	As Followers, Sojourners	As Servants, Ambassadors
Christian Worldview	Communal Identity	Spiritual Experience	Biblical Authority	Orthodox Theology	Priestly Worship	Congregational Discipleship	Kingdom Witness
Theistic and Trinitarian Vision	Christ-centered Foundation	Spirit-Indwelt and -Filled Community	Canonical and Apostolic Witness	Ancient Creedal Affirmation of Faith	Weekly Gathering in Christian Assembly	Corporate, Ongoing Spiritual Formation	Active Agents of the Reign of God
Sovereign Willing	Messianic Representing	Divine Comforting	Inspired Testifying	Truthful Retelling	Joyful Excelling	Faithful Indwelling	Hopeful Compelling
Creator — True Maker of the Cosmos	Recapitulation — Typos and Fulfillment of the Covenant	Life-Giver — Regeneration and Adoption	Divine Inspiration — God-breathed Word	The Confession of Faith — Union with Christ	Song and Celebration — Historical Recitation	Pastoral Oversight — Shepherding the Flock	Explicit Unity — Love for the Saints
Owner — Sovereign Disposer of Creation	Revealer — Incarnation of the Word	Teacher — Illuminator of the Truth	Sacred History — Historical Record	Baptism into Christ — Communion of Saints	Homilies and Teachings — Prophetic Proclamation	Shared Spirituality — Common Journey through the Spiritual Disciplines	Radical Hospitality — Evidence of God's Kingdom Reign
Ruler — Blessed Controller of All Things	Redeemer — Reconciler of All Things	Helper — Endowment and the Power	Biblical Theology — Divine Commentary	The Rule of Faith — Apostles' Creed and Nicene Creed	The Lord's Supper — Dramatic Re-enactment	Embodiment — Anamnesis and Prolepsis through the Church Year	Extravagant Generosity — Good Works
Covenant Keeper — Faithful Promisor	Restorer — Christ, the Victor over the powers of evil	Guide — Divine Presence and Shekinah	Spiritual Food — Sustenance for the Journey	The Vincentian Canon — Ubiquity, antiquity, universality	Eschatological Foreshadowing — The Already/Not Yet	Effective Discipling — Spiritual Formation in the Believing Assembly	Evangelical Witness — Making Disciples of All People Groups

APPENDIX 16

Handing Down the Apostolic Deposit
Passing Down the Story through Discipleship and Tradition

Rev. Dr. Don L. Davis

Guard the Good Deposit

Follow the pattern of the sound words that you have heard from me, in the faith and love that are in Christ Jesus. By the Holy Spirit who dwells within us, guard the good deposit entrusted to you.
~ 2 Tim. 1.13-14

You, however, have followed my teaching, my conduct, my aim in life, my faith, my patience, my love, my steadfastness, my persecutions and sufferings that happened to me at Antioch, at Iconium, and at Lystra—which persecutions I endured; yet from them all the Lord rescued me.
~ 2 Tim. 3.10-11

Protect the Entrusted Story

O Timothy, guard the deposit entrusted to you. Avoid the irreverent babble and contradictions of what is falsely called "knowledge"
~1 Tim. 6.20

Now we command you, brothers, in the name of our Lord Jesus Christ, that you keep away from any brother who is walking in idleness and not in accord with the tradition that you received from us.
~ 2 Thess. 3.6

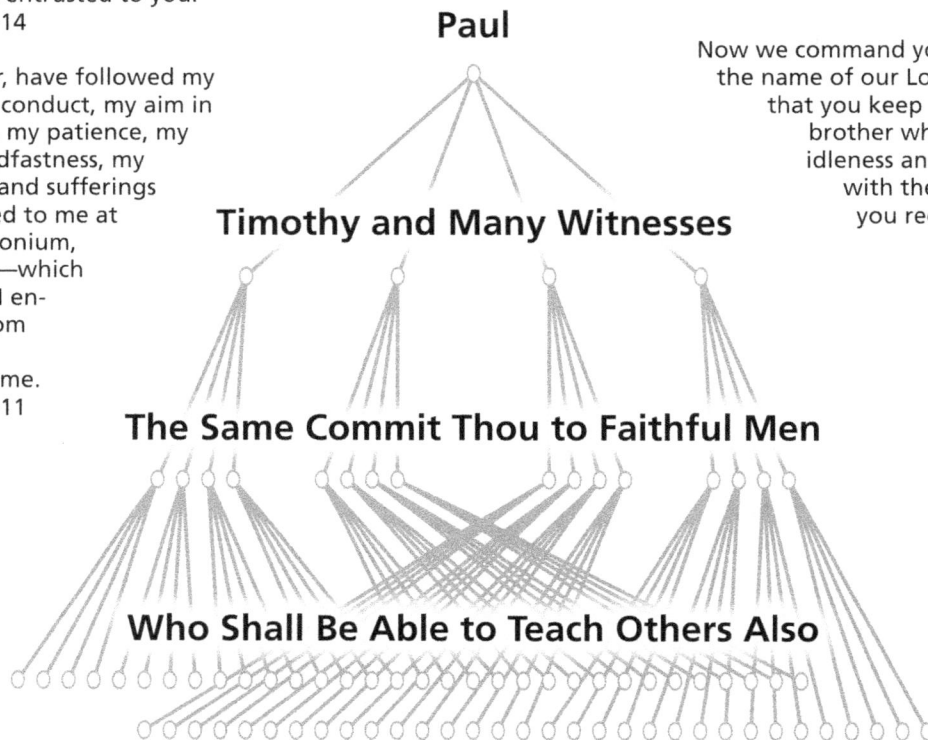

Paul

Timothy and Many Witnesses

The Same Commit Thou to Faithful Men

Who Shall Be Able to Teach Others Also

2 Tim. 2.2 (ESV) – And what you have heard from me in the presence of many witnesses entrust to faithful men who will be able to teach others also.

The key to multiplying disciples is equipping others with the very story, truths, practices, and traditions which the apostles handed down to their faithful disciples, who in obedience to Christ passed them down through the generations, even to us.

What is the center of this tradition? It is the story of God's saving actions in Christ – his coming, incarnation, passion, crucifixion, burial, resurrection, ascension, session, and second Coming. They were eyewitnesses of his Majesty, and commanded his church to walk worthy of their calling, testifying in word and deed of the hope of his return. To disciple is to ground people in this Story of God in Christ in the midst of Christian assembly, expressed in a shared spirituality and through a common identity – in worship, faith, service, and witness.

APPENDIX 17

Christus Victor
An Integrated Vision for the Christian Life and Witness
Rev. Dr. Don L. Davis

For the Church
- The Church is the primary extension of Jesus in the world
- Ransomed treasure of the victorious, risen Christ
- *Laos:* The people of God
- God's new creation: presence of the future
- Locus and agent of the Already/Not Yet Kingdom

For Gifts
- God's gracious endowments and benefits from *Christus Victor*
- Pastoral offices to the Church
- The Holy Spirit's sovereign dispensing of the gifts
- Stewardship: divine, diverse gifts for the common good

For Theology and Doctrine
- The authoritative Word of Christ's victory: the Apostolic Tradition: the Holy Scriptures
- Theology as commentary on the grand narrative of God
- *Christus Victor* as core theological framework for meaning in the world
- The Nicene Creed: the Story of God's triumphant grace

Christus Victor
Destroyer of Evil and Death
Restorer of Creation
Victor o'er Hades and Sin
Crusher of Satan

For Spirituality
- The Holy Spirit's presence and power in the midst of God's people
- Sharing in the disciplines of the Spirit
- Gatherings, lectionary, liturgy, and our observances in the Church Year
- Living the life of the risen Christ in the rhythm of our ordinary lives

For Worship
- People of the Resurrection: unending celebration of the people of God
- Remembering, participating in the Christ event in our worship
- Listen and respond to the Word
- Transformed at the Table, the Lord's Supper
- The presence of the Father through the Son in the Spirit

For Evangelism and Mission
- Evangelism as unashamed declaration and demonstration of *Christus Victor* to the world
- The Gospel as Good News of kingdom pledge
- We proclaim God's Kingdom come in the person of Jesus of Nazareth
- The Great Commission: go to all people groups making disciples of Christ and his Kingdom
- Proclaiming Christ as Lord and Messiah

For Justice and Compassion
- The gracious and generous expressions of Jesus through the Church
- The Church displays the very life of the Kingdom
- The Church demonstrates the very life of the Kingdom of heaven right here and now
- Having freely received, we freely give (no sense of merit or pride)
- Justice as tangible evidence of the Kingdom come

APPENDIX 18

The Theology of Christus Victor

Rev. Dr. Don L. Davis

	The Promised Messiah	The Word Made Flesh	The Son of Man	The Suffering Servant	The Lamb of God	The Victorious Conqueror	The Reigning Lord in Heaven	The Bridegroom and Coming King
Biblical Framework	Israel's hope of Yahweh's anointed who would redeem his people	In the person of Jesus of Nazareth, the Lord has come to the world	As the promised king and divine Son of Man, Jesus reveals the Father's glory and salvation to the world	As Inaugurator of the Kingdom of God, Jesus demonstrates God's reign present through his words, wonders, and works	As both High Priest and Paschal Lamb, Jesus offers himself to God on our behalf as a sacrifice for sin	In his resurrection from the dead and ascension to God's right hand, Jesus is proclaimed as Victor over the power of sin and death	Now reigning at God's right hand till his enemies are made his footstool, Jesus pours out his benefits on his body	Soon the risen and ascended Lord will return to gather his Bride, the Church, and consummate his work
Scripture References	Isa. 9.6-7 Jer. 23.5-6 Isa. 11.1-10	John 1.14-18 Matt. 1.20-23 Phil. 2.6-8	Matt. 2.1-11 Num. 24.17 Luke 1.78-79	Mark 1.14-15 Matt. 12.25-30 Luke 17.20-21	2 Cor. 5.18-21 Isa. 52-53 John 1.29	Eph. 1.16-23 Phil. 2.5-11 Col. 1.15-20	1 Cor. 15.25 Eph. 4.15-16 Acts. 2.32-36	Rom. 14.7-9 Rev. 5.9-13 1 Thess. 4.13-18
Jesus' History	The pre-incarnate, only begotten Son of God in glory	His conception by the Spirit, and birth to Mary	His manifestation to the Magi and to the world	His teaching, exorcisms, miracles, and mighty works among the people	His suffering, crucifixion, death, and burial	His resurrection, with appearances to his witnesses, and his ascension to the Father	The sending of the Holy Spirit and his gifts, and Christ's session in heaven at the Father's right hand	His soon return from heaven to earth as Lord and Christ: the Second Coming
Description	The biblical promise for the seed of Abraham, the prophet like Moses, the son of David	In the Incarnation, God has come to us; Jesus reveals to humankind the Father's glory in fullness	In Jesus, God has shown his salvation to the entire world, including the Gentiles	In Jesus, the promised Kingdom of God has come visibly to earth, demonstrating his binding of Satan and rescinding the Curse	As God's perfect Lamb, Jesus offers himself up to God as a sin offering on behalf of the entire world	In his resurrection and ascension, Jesus destroyed death, disarmed Satan, and rescinded the Curse	Jesus is installed at the Father's right hand as Head of the Church, Firstborn from the dead, and supreme Lord in heaven	As we labor in his harvest field in the world, so we await Christ's return, the fulfillment of his promise
Church Year	Advent	Christmas	Season after Epiphany Baptism and Transfiguration	Lent	Holy Week Passion	Eastertide Easter, Ascension Day, Pentecost	Season after Pentecost Trinity Sunday	Season after Pentecost All Saints Day, Reign of Christ the King
	The Coming of Christ	*The Birth of Christ*	*The Manifestation of Christ*	*The Ministry of Christ*	*The Suffering and Death of Christ*	*The Resurrection and Ascension of Christ*	*The Heavenly Session of Christ*	*The Reign of Christ*
Spiritual Formation	As we await his Coming, let us proclaim and affirm the hope of Christ	O Word made flesh, let us every heart prepare him room to dwell	Divine Son of Man, show the nations your salvation and glory	In the person of Christ, the power of the reign of God has come to earth and to the Church	May those who share the Lord's death be resurrected with him	Let us participate by faith in the victory of Christ over the power of sin, Satan, and death	Come, indwell us, Holy Spirit, and empower us to advance Christ's Kingdom in the world	We live and work in expectation of his soon return, seeking to please him in all things

APPENDIX 19

Jesus of Nazareth: The Presence of the Future

Rev. Dr. Don L. Davis

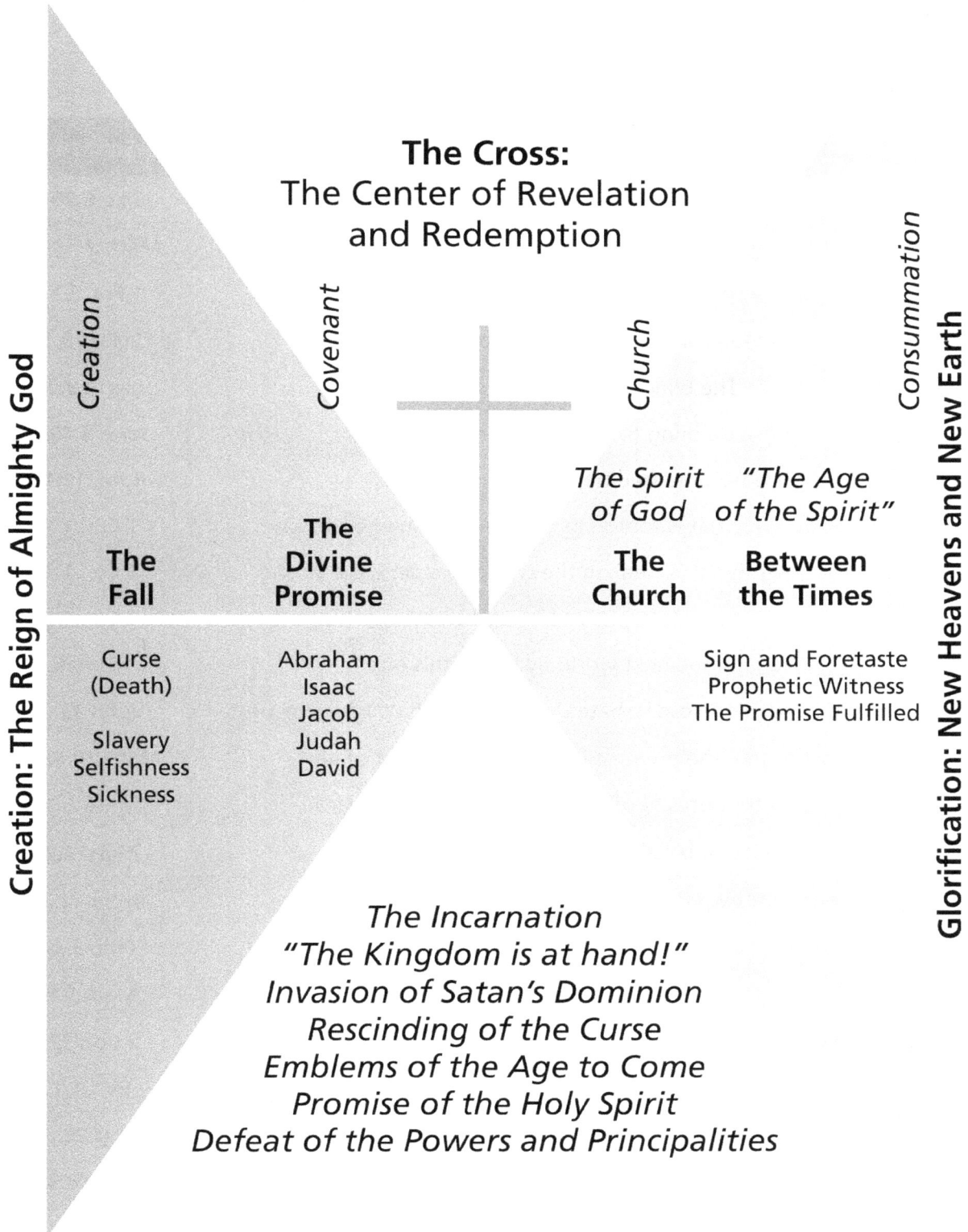

Creation: The Reign of Almighty God

Glorification: New Heavens and New Earth

Creation

Covenant

Church

Consummation

The Cross:
The Center of Revelation and Redemption

The Spirit of God   *"The Age of the Spirit"*

The Fall

The Divine Promise

The Church

Between the Times

Curse (Death)

Slavery
Selfishness
Sickness

Abraham
Isaac
Jacob
Judah
David

Sign and Foretaste
Prophetic Witness
The Promise Fulfilled

The Incarnation
"The Kingdom is at hand!"
Invasion of Satan's Dominion
Rescinding of the Curse
Emblems of the Age to Come
Promise of the Holy Spirit
Defeat of the Powers and Principalities

APPENDIX 20
Ethics of the New Testament
Living in the Upside-Down Kingdom of God – True Myth and Biblical Fairy Tale
Rev. Dr. Don L. Davis

The Principle of Reversal

The Principle Expressed	Scripture
The poor shall become rich, and the rich shall become poor	Luke 6.20-26
The law breaker and the undeserving are saved	Matt. 21.31-32
Those who humble themselves shall be exalted	1 Pet. 5.5-6
Those who exalt themselves shall be brought low	Luke 18.14
The blind shall be given sight	John 9.39
Those claiming to see shall be made blind	John 9.40-41
We become free by being Christ's slave	Rom. 12.1-2
God has chosen what is foolish in the world to shame the wise	1 Cor. 1.27
God has chosen what is weak in the world to shame the strong	1 Cor. 1.27
God has chosen the low and despised to bring to nothing things that are	1 Cor. 1.28
We gain the next world by losing this one	1 Tim. 6.7
Love this life and you'll lose it; hate this life, and you'll keep the next	John 12.25
You become the greatest by being the servant of all	Matt. 10.42-45
Store up treasures here, you forfeit heaven's reward	Matt. 6.19
Store up treasures above, you gain heaven's wealth	Matt. 6.20
Accept your own death to yourself in order to live fully	John 12.24
Release all earthly reputation to gain heaven's favor	Phil. 3.3-7
The first shall be last, and the last shall become first	Mark 9.35
The grace of Jesus is perfected in your weakness, not your strength	2 Cor. 12.9
God's highest sacrifice is contrition and brokenness	Ps. 51.17
It is better to give to others than to receive from them	Acts 20.35
Give away all you have in order to receive God's best	Luke 6.38

A Call to an Ancient Evangelical Future

Revised 36-5.12.06

Prologue

In every age the Holy Spirit calls the Church to examine its faithfulness to God's revelation in Jesus Christ, authoritatively recorded in Scripture and handed down through the Church. Thus, while we affirm the global strength and vitality of worldwide Evangelicalism in our day, we believe the North American expression of Evangelicalism needs to be especially sensitive to the new external and internal challenges facing God's people.

These external challenges include the current cultural milieu and the resurgence of religious and political ideologies. The internal challenges include Evangelical accommodation to civil religion, rationalism, privatism and pragmatism. In light of these challenges, we call Evangelicals to strengthen their witness through a recovery of the faith articulated by the consensus of the ancient Church and its guardians in the traditions of Eastern Orthodoxy, Roman Catholicism, the Protestant Reformation and the Evangelical awakenings. Ancient Christians faced a world of paganism, Gnosticism and political domination. In the face of heresy and persecution, they understood history through Israel's story, culminating in the death and resurrection of Jesus and the coming of God's Kingdom.

Today, as in the ancient era, the Church is confronted by a host of master narratives that contradict and compete with the gospel. The pressing question is: who gets to narrate the world? The *Call to an Ancient Evangelical Future* challenges Evangelical Christians to restore the priority of the divinely inspired biblical story of God's acts in history. The narrative of God's Kingdom holds eternal implications for the mission of the Church, its theological reflection, its public ministries of worship and spirituality and its life in the world. By engaging these themes, we believe the Church will be strengthened to address the issues of our day.

1. On the Primacy of the Biblical Narrative

We call for a return to the priority of the divinely authorized canonical story of the Triune God. This story – Creation, Incarnation, and Re-creation – was effected by Christ's recapitulation of human history and summarized by the early Church in its Rules of Faith. The gospel-formed content of these Rules served as the key to the interpretation of Scripture and its critique of contemporary culture, and thus shaped the church's pastoral ministry. Today, we call Evangelicals to turn away from modern

A Call to an Ancient Evangelical Future, continued

theological methods that reduce the gospel to mere propositions, and from contemporary pastoral ministries so compatible with culture that they camouflage God's story or empty it of its cosmic and redemptive meaning. In a world of competing stories, we call Evangelicals to recover the truth of God's word as the story of the world, and to make it the centerpiece of Evangelical life.

2. On the Church, the Continuation of God's Narrative

We call Evangelicals to take seriously the visible character of the Church. We call for a commitment to its mission in the world in fidelity to God's mission (*Missio Dei*), and for an exploration of the ecumenical implications this has for the unity, holiness catholicity, and apostolicity of the Church. Thus, we call Evangelicals to turn away from an individualism that makes the Church a mere addendum to God's redemptive plan. Individualistic Evangelicalism has contributed to the current problems of churchless Christianity, redefinitions of the Church according to business models, separatist ecclesiologies and judgmental attitudes toward the Church. Therefore, we call Evangelicals to recover their place in the community of the Church catholic.

3. On the Church's Theological Reflection on God's Narrative

We call for the Church's reflection to remain anchored in the Scriptures in continuity with the theological interpretation learned from the early Fathers. Thus, we call Evangelicals to turn away from methods that separate theological reflection from the common traditions of the Church. These modern methods compartmentalize God's story by analyzing its separate parts, while ignoring God's entire redemptive work as recapitulated in Christ. Anti-historical attitudes also disregard the common biblical and theological legacy of the ancient Church. Such disregard ignores the hermeneutical value of the Church's ecumenical creeds. This reduces God's story of the world to one of many competing theologies and impairs the unified witness of the Church to God's plan for the history of the world. Therefore, we call Evangelicals to unity in "the tradition that has been believed everywhere, always and by all," as well as to humility and charity in their various Protestant traditions.

4. On Church's Worship as Telling and Enacting God's Narrative

We call for public worship that sings, preaches and enacts God's story. We call for a renewed consideration of how God ministers to us in baptism, eucharist, confession, the laying on of hands, marriage, healing and through the charisms of the Spirit, for these actions shape our lives and signify the meaning of the world. Thus, we call Evangelicals to turn away from forms of worship that focus on God as a mere object of the intellect, or that assert the self as the source of worship. Such worship

A Call to an Ancient Evangelical Future, continued

has resulted in lecture-oriented, music-driven, performance-centered and program-controlled models that do not adequately proclaim God's cosmic redemption. Therefore, we call Evangelicals to recover the historic substance of worship of Word and Table and to attend to the Christian year, which marks time according to God's saving acts.

5. On Spiritual Formation in the Church as Embodiment of God's Narrative

We call for a catechetical spiritual formation of the people of God that is based firmly on a Trinitarian biblical narrative. We are concerned when spirituality is separated from the story of God and baptism into the life of Christ and his Body. Spirituality, made independent from God's story, is often characterized by legalism, mere intellectual knowledge, an overly therapeutic culture, New Age Gnosticism, a dualistic rejection of this world and a narcissistic preoccupation with one's own experience. These false spiritualities are inadequate for the challenges we face in today's world. Therefore, we call Evangelicals to return to a historic spirituality like that taught and practiced in the ancient catechumenate.

6. On the Church's Embodied Life in the World

We call for a cruciform holiness and commitment to God's mission in the world. This embodied holiness affirms life, biblical morality and appropriate self-denial. It calls us to be faithful stewards of the created order and bold prophets to our contemporary culture. Thus, we call Evangelicals to intensify their prophetic voice against forms of indifference to God's gift of life, economic and political injustice, ecological insensitivity and the failure to champion the poor and marginalized. Too often we have failed to stand prophetically against the culture's captivity to racism, consumerism, political correctness, civil religion, sexism, ethical relativism, violence and the culture of death. These failures have muted the voice of Christ to the world through his Church and detract from God's story of the world, which the Church is collectively to embody. Therefore, we call the Church to recover its counter-cultural mission to the world.

Epilogue

In sum, we call Evangelicals to recover the conviction that God's story shapes the mission of the Church to bear witness to God's Kingdom and to inform the spiritual foundations of civilization. We set forth this *Call* as an ongoing, open-ended conversation. We are aware that we have our blind spots and weaknesses. Therefore, we encourage Evangelicals to engage this *Call* within educational centers, denominations and local churches through publications and conferences.

A Call to an Ancient Evangelical Future, continued

We pray that we can move with intention to proclaim a loving, transcendent, triune God who has become involved in our history. In line with Scripture, creed and tradition, it is our deepest desire to embody God's purposes in the mission of the Church through our theological reflection, our worship, our spirituality and our life in the world, all the while proclaiming that Jesus is Lord over all creation.

© Northern Seminary 2006 Robert Webber and Phil Kenyon Permission is granted to reproduce the *Call* in unaltered form with proper citation.

Sponsors
Northern Seminary (*www.seminary.edu*)
Baker Books (*www.bakerbooks.com*)
Institute for Worship Studies (*www.iwsfla.org*)
InterVarsity Press (*www.ivpress.com*)

This *Call* is issued in the spirit of *sic et non*; therefore those who affix their names to this *Call* need not agree with all its content. Rather, its consensus is that these are issues to be discussed in the tradition of *semper reformanda* as the church faces the new challenges of our time. Over a period of seven months, more than 300 persons have participated via e-mail to write the *Call*. These men and women represent a broad diversity of ethnicity and denominational affiliation. The four theologians who most consistently interacted with the development of the *Call* have been named as Theological Editors. The Board of Reference was given the special assignment of overall approval.

If you wish to be a signer on the *Call* go to *www.ancientfutureworship.com*

APPENDIX 22

Rapid Church Multiplication
The Elements of Dynamic Church Planting Movements
Rev. Dr. Don L. Davis

Elements of Dynamic Church Planting Movements				
Elements	Shared Spirituality	People Group Identity	Dynamic Standardization	Level of Fruitfulness
Meaning	*Vital Spiritual Formation*	*Compelling Translation*	*Efficient Systemization*	
Definition	Possessing a common spiritual identity in a church body that expresses the Great Tradition	Affirming our freedom in Christ to embody the faith within ethnicity and culture	Rapidly reproducing healthy churches of a kind through shared protocols and resources	
Explanation	Presumes a valid, distinctive apostolic spiritual identity embodied in a church body (why and what)	Conditions how that identity is understood, practiced (where and with whom)	Determines how that identity is formed, nourished, and multiplied (how)	
Burden	To express a common spiritual vision and discipline in shared practice	To contextualize within a culture or people group	To organize and coordinate resources for the common good	
Alternative Approaches in Church Planting — Model 1	Communal bond built on kindred spiritual practice	Full embodiment in receiving culture	Integrated structures and common protocols	*Most Effective*
Model 2	Same shared elements of spirituality and practice	More attention to culture and ethnicity	Voluntary structures and optional protocols	*More Effective*
Model 3	Divergent, dissimilar spirituality and practice	Some attention to culture and ethnicity	Iconoclastic structures and divergent protocols	*Less Effective*
Model 4	Fragmented approaches to spirituality and practice	No attention to culture and ethnicity	Arbitrary structures and random protocols	*Least Effective*

History and Identity (*Our Common Heritage*)
Our church planting movements must link themselves to and identify with themselves by a well defined and joyfully shared history and persona that all members and congregations share.

Membership and Belonging (*Our Common Discipline*)
Our church planting movements must be anchored in evangelical and historically orthodox presentations of the Gospel that results in conversions to Jesus Christ and incorporation into local churches.

Theology and Doctrine (*Our Common Faith*)

Our church planting movements must be anchored in a common theology and Christian education (catechism) that reflects a commonly held faith.

Worship and Liturgy (*Our Common Worship*)

Our church planting movements must reflect a shared hymnody, liturgy, symbology, and spiritual formation that enables us to worship and glorify God in such a way that lifts up the Lord and attracts urbanites to vital worship.

Convocation and Association (*Our Common Partnership*)

Our church planting movements must seek to connect, link, and associate the congregations and leaders within our movement to one another in regular communication, fellowship, and alliance.

Justice and Support Ministries (*Our Common Service*)

Our church planting movements must demonstrate the love and justice of the Kingdom in the city in practical ways that allow individuals and congregations to love their neighbors as they love themselves.

Resources and Finances (*Our Common Stewardship*)

Our church planting movements must handle their financial affairs and resources with wise, streamlined, and reproducible policies that allow for the good management of our monies and resources.

Church Government (*Our Common Polity*)

Our church planting movements must be organized around a common polity, management, and governing policies that allow for efficient management of our resources and congregations.

Leadership Development Policies and Strategies (*Our Common Shepherding*)

Our church planting movements must be committed to identifying, equipping, and supporting pastors and missionaries in our congregations that links all of our leaders to one another in faith and practice.

Evangelism and Missions (*Our Common Mission*)

Our church planting movements must coordinate their efforts and activities around giving clear witness of Jesus to the city and results in significant numbers of new congregations being planted and joining our movement as quickly as possible.

APPENDIX 23

Understanding and Practice of Church Planting Movement Principles

Rev. Dr. Don L. Davis

Critical CPM Principles

1. Shared spirituality and identity
2. People-group contextualization
3. Dynamic standardization

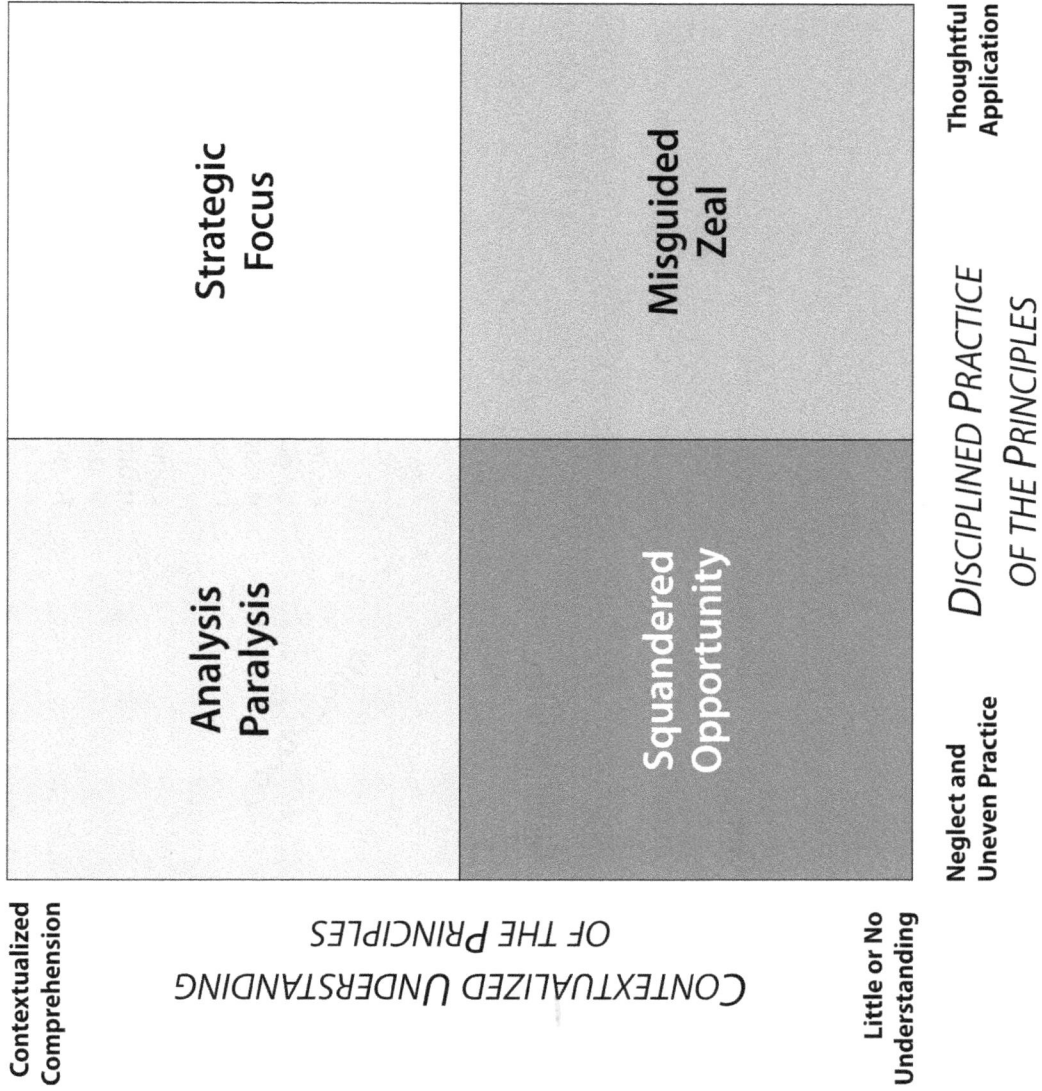

Analysis Paralysis	Strategic Focus
Squandered Opportunity	Misguided Zeal

Contextualized Comprehension

Little or No Understanding

CONTEXTUALIZED UNDERSTANDING OF THE PRINCIPLES

Neglect and Uneven Practice

Thoughtful Application

DISCIPLINED PRACTICE OF THE PRINCIPLES

APPENDIX 24

The Threefold Cord of Urban Cross-Cultural Church Planting Movements

Rev. Dr. Don L. Davis

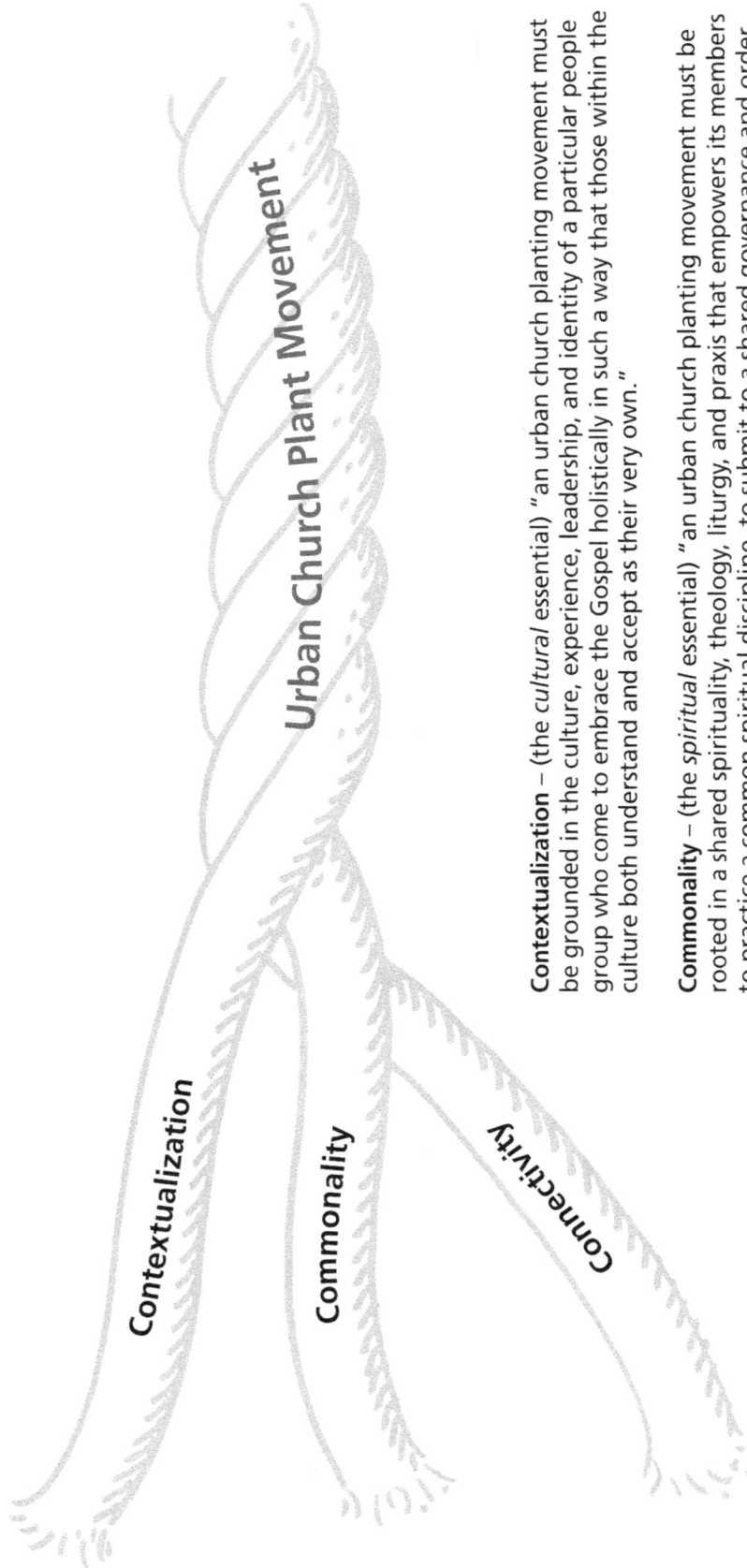

Urban Church Plant Movement

Contextualization

Commonality

Connectivity

Ecc. 4.12 (ESV) - And though a man might prevail against one who is alone, two will withstand him – a threefold cord is not quickly broken.

Contextualization – (the *cultural essential*) "an urban church planting movement must be grounded in the culture, experience, leadership, and identity of a particular people group who come to embrace the Gospel holistically in such a way that those within the culture both understand and accept as their very own."

Commonality – (the *spiritual essential*) "an urban church planting movement must be rooted in a shared spirituality, theology, liturgy, and praxis that empowers its members to practice a common spiritual discipline, to submit to a shared governance and order, to recognize and affirm its unique theological and spiritual distinctives, to incorporate and confirm its members and leaders according to a common protocol, and to integrate the efforts of its congregations together into a coherent, unified movement."

Connectivity – (the *structural essential*) "an urban church planting movement must connect its leaders, members, and congregations through integrated structures that enable its congregations and leaders to gather regularly for convocation and fellowship, that combine resources and funds for cooperation and mutual support, and that provide oversight that protects and equips the members of the movement for dynamic reproduction."

World Impact's Church Planting Schema and the Pauline Cycle

World Impact and David J. Hesselgrave

Pauline Precedents from Acts: The Pauline Cycle

1. Missionaries Commissioned: Acts 13.1-4; 15.39-40; Gal. 1.15-16.

2. Audience Contacted: Acts 13.14-16; 14.1; 16.13-15; 17.16-19.

3. Gospel Communicated: Acts 13.17-41; 16.31; Rom. 10.9-14; 2 Tim. 2.8.

4. Hearers Converted: Acts. 13.48; 16.14-15; 20.21; 26.20; 1 Thess. 1.9-10.

5. Believers Congregated: Acts 13.43; 19.9; Rom 16.4-5; 1 Cor. 14.26.

6. Faith Confirmed: Acts 14.21-22; 15.41; Rom 16.17; Col. 1.28; 2 Thess. 2.15; 1 Tim. 1.3.

7. Leadership Consecrated; Acts 14.23; 2 Tim. 2.2; Titus 1.5.

8. Believers Commended; Acts 14.23; 16.40; 21.32 (2 Tim. 4.9 and Titus 3.12 by implication).

9. Relationships Continued: Acts 15.36; 18.23; 1 Cor. 16.5; Eph. 6.21-22; Col. 4.7-8.

10. Sending Churches Convened: Acts 14.26-27; 15.1-4.

APPENDIX 26

The Interaction of Class, Culture, and Race

Rev. Dr. Don L. Davis

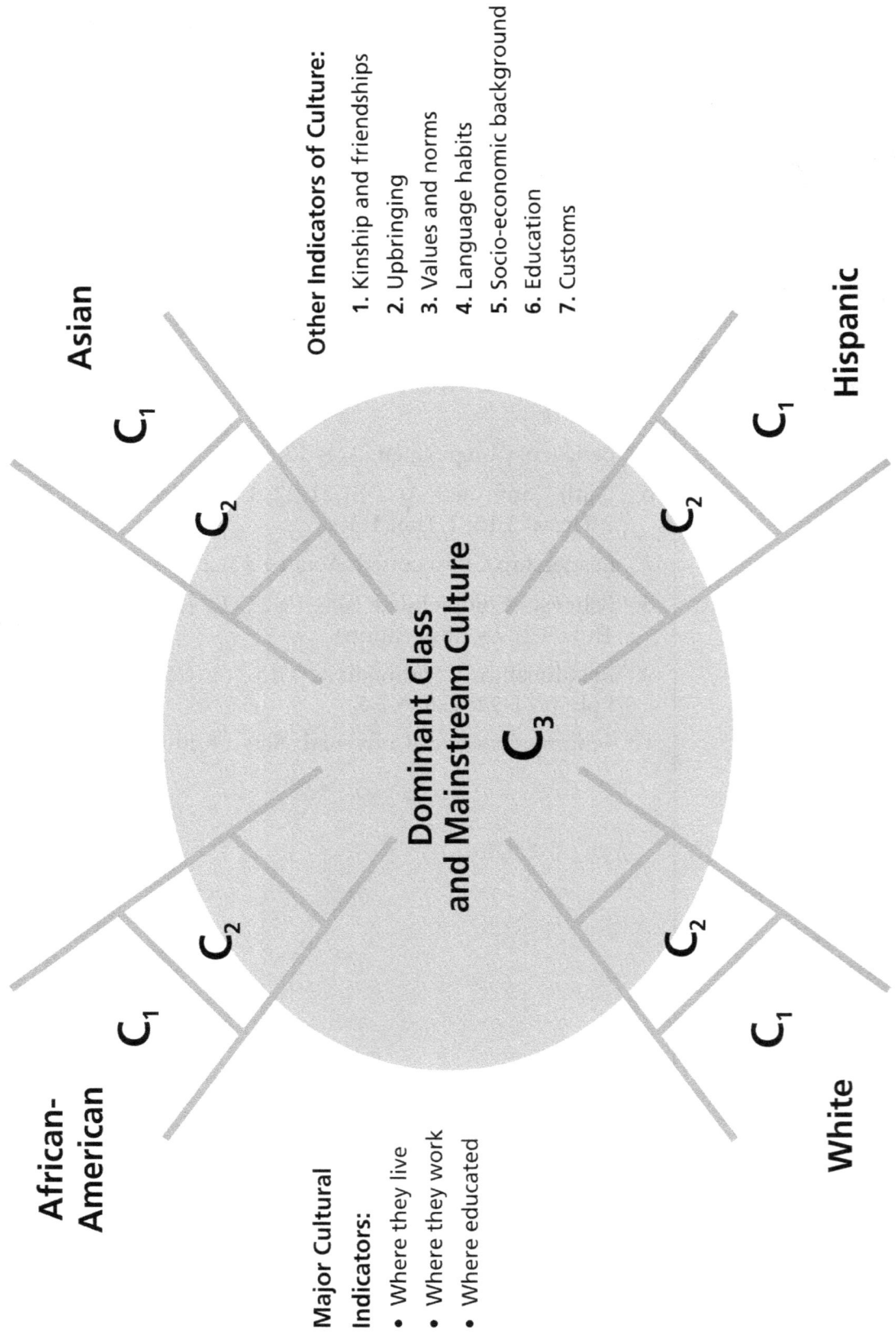

Other Indicators of Culture:

1. Kinship and friendships
2. Upbringing
3. Values and norms
4. Language habits
5. Socio-economic background
6. Education
7. Customs

Major Cultural Indicators:

- Where they live
- Where they work
- Where educated

Asian

Hispanic

African-American

White

C_1

C_2

C_3

Dominant Class and Mainstream Culture

APPENDIX 27

The Complexity of Difference: Race, Culture, Class

Rev. Dr. Don L. Davis

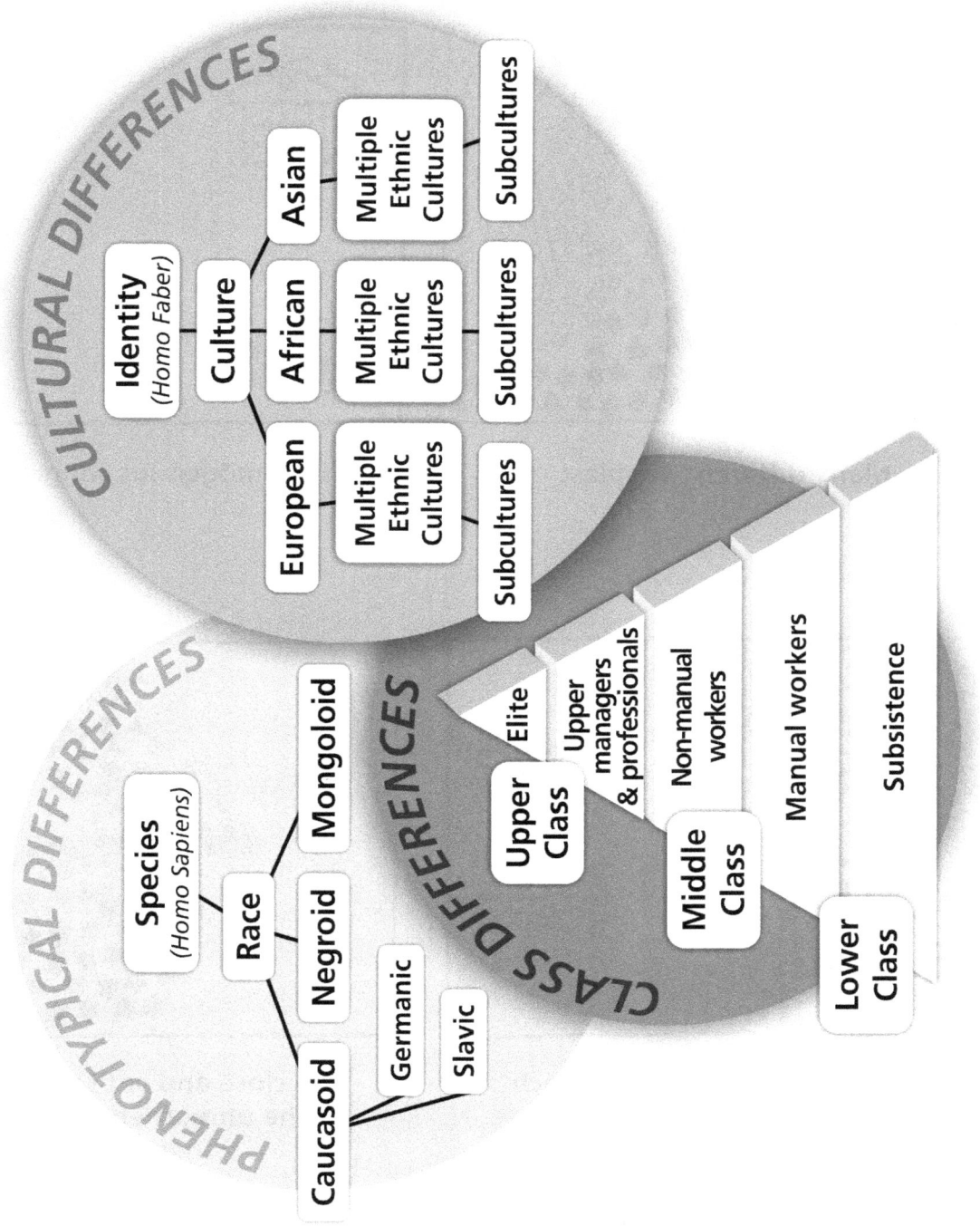

CULTURAL DIFFERENCES

Identity
(Homo Faber)

Culture

European — African — Asian

Multiple Ethnic Cultures — Multiple Ethnic Cultures — Multiple Ethnic Cultures

Subcultures — Subcultures — Subcultures

PHENOTYPICAL DIFFERENCES

Species
(Homo Sapiens)

Race

Caucasoid — Negroid — Mongoloid

Germanic — Slavic

CLASS DIFFERENCES

Elite

Upper Class

Upper managers & professionals

Non-manual workers

Middle Class

Manual workers

Lower Class

Subsistence

Targeting Unreached Groups in Churched Neighborhoods
Rev. Dr. Don L. Davis

Many different peoples!

Many homogenous congregations.

**The extent of normal "outreach":
Incorporating and gathering
according to culture.**

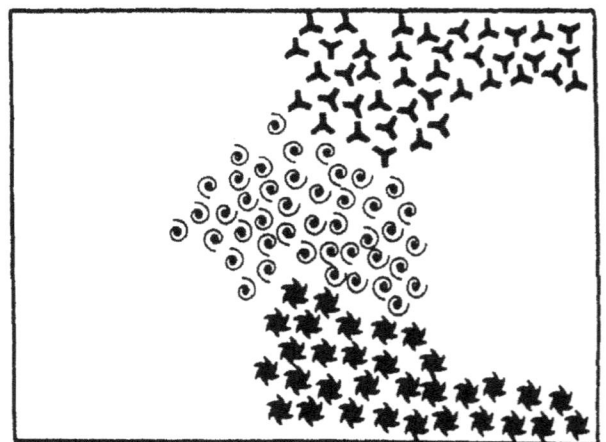

**"So close and yet so far away":
The unreached, unaffected
neighbors.**

APPENDIX 29

Ten Key Cross-Cultural Church Planting Principles
World Impact

1. **Jesus is Lord.** (Matt. 9.37-38) All church plant activity is made effective and fruitful under the watch care and power of the Lord Jesus, who himself is the Lord of the harvest.

2. **Evangelize, Equip, and Empower unreached people to reach people.** (1 Thess. 1.6-8) Our goal in reaching others for Christ is not only for solid conversion but also for dynamic multiplication; those who are reached must be trained to reach others as well.

3. **Be inclusive: whosoever will may come.** (Rom. 10.12) No strategy should forbid any person or group from entering into the Kingdom through Jesus Christ by faith.

4. **Be culturally neutral: Come just as you are.** (Col. 3.11) The Gospel places no demands on any seeker to change their culture as a prerequisite for coming to Jesus; they may come just as they are.

5. **Avoid a fortress mentality.** (Acts 1.8) The goal of missions is not to create an impregnable castle in the midst of an unsaved community, but a dynamic outpost of the Kingdom which launches a witness for Jesus within and unto the very borders of their world.

6. **Continue to evangelize to avoid stagnation.** (Rom. 1.16-17) Keep looking to the horizons with the vision of the Great Commission in mind; foster an environment of aggressive witness for Christ.

7. **Cross racial, class, gender, and language barriers.** (1 Cor. 9.19-22) Use your freedom in Christ to find new, credible ways to communicate the kingdom message to those farthest from the cultural spectrum of the traditional church.

8. **Respect the dominance of the receiving culture.** (Acts 15.23-29) Allow the Holy Spirit to incarnate the vision and the ethics of the Kingdom of God in the words, language, customs, styles, and experience of those who have embraced Jesus as their Lord.

9. **Avoid dependence.** (Eph. 4.11-16) Neither patronize nor be overly stingy towards the growing congregation; do not underestimate the power of the Spirit in the midst of even the smallest Christian community to accomplish God's work in their community.

10. **Think reproducibility.** (2 Tim. 2.2; Phil. 1.18) In every activity and project you initiate, think in terms of equipping others to do the same by maintaining an open mind regarding the means and ends of your missionary endeavors.

APPENDIX 30

Resourcing the Great Commission
The Three Contexts of TUMI Resources and Partnerships

Rev. Dr. Don L. Davis

Contexts of Resourcing and Partnership	Summary	Key Conception
Context One *The One Call to Make Disciples of Christ: The Great Commission*	Matt. 28.18-20; Mark 16.15-16; Luke 24.44-48; John 20.21-23	The Great Commission is the charge to reach the vast number of doomed souls in eternal peril with the Gospel of salvation and transformation as authentically and quickly as possible among all peoples. →
Context Two *The Two Major Agents of Kingdom Display: Movements and Congregations*	1 Tim. 3.15-16	
Movements, Denominations, Missions Organizations, Gospel Ministries	Trueblood's "Company of the Committed"; the basic unit of kingdom display and witness – a credible church movement, planting churches within a particular people and locale	A discrete company in God's Kingdom Army, raised up by the Spirit to represent the Kingdom in a unique, particular, and discernible place and population
Local Congregations (pastorally led assemblies of Christ followers)	Local, concrete outpost of the Kingdom in a specific locale, neighborhood, under the auspices, instruction, and authority of a credible church movement	A platoon, connected to a particular company, raised up by the Spirit to represent the Kingdom in the company's spirit and name, to engage people as to help them be formed according to the three stages of spiritual formation in a local assembly →
Context Three *The Three Stages of Spiritual Formation: Evangelism, Discipleship, and Commission*	Eph. 4.9-15; Col. 1.28-29	
From Sincere Seeker to Baptized Believer *Communicating the Good News to Open Hearts*	Credible communication of the Good News leading to repentance and confession of Christ, and baptism, connected to a local assembly and its life together	Culturally conducive, effective evangelism (sharing the Good News) of God's love in Christ that results in saving faith and baptism in connection to an authentic assembly of Christ followers under pastoral care
From Baptized Believer to Maturing Disciple/Body Member *Equipping Baptized Believers to live the Christian life in kingdom community*	Incorporation of a baptized believer into official, formal, and genuine relationship with a local congregation, under pastoral care and supervision, integrated in its life and witness	Ongoing process of integrating a baptized believer into the life and witness of a local church, involving nurturing spiritual formation, meaningful worship, dynamic fellowship, and spiritual witness to people within their *oikos* network of family, friends, and associates →
From Maturing Disciple/Body Member to Commissioned Minister *Maturing disciples commissioned by the laying on of hands of pastor and elders to engage in outreach, ministry, and witness to those within their oikos and their calling* *Clergy: formal class/category of official pastoral authority certified by the congregation or the movement* *Lay Minister: commissioning and releasing mature disciples to serve as ambassadors in their respective contexts, undergirded with prayer, authority, and resources from their assembly*	Enabling growing, maturing disciples/body members to discover their gifts and find opportunities to serve as laborers in their own unique, Holy Spirit led field of *oikos* and/or their specific call to ministry	Identifying, equipping, and releasing empowered urban Christian leaders to minister and Christ's ambassadors in their Spirit-led context (*Sitz im leben*), i.e., their circle of family, friends, and associates, and to their specific called group for witness (e.g., Paul's call to the Gentiles)

Biblical Image	Suggested TUMI Resources	WI Staff and Associate Roles
Laborers in the harvest field	All TUMI resources connect to the fulfillment of the Great Commission's charge to make disciples of all nations (i.e., the universal priesthood of believers)	World Impact Staff and Associates serve as Area Specialists, experts in training and referring leaders and churches by need, by age, by process, or by resource
The role of the Tribes in Israel, i.e., particular tribes of the singular nation (e.g., the Churches of Macedonia)	**Note: TUMI resources and consultations are informed by biblical models and analogies of birth, growth, maturity, and fruitfulness (systems thinking) of our conversion and calling.**	**Note: WI Staff and Associates are charged to identify, equip, and release urban Christian leaders to spawn and strengthen indigenous movements and congregations to fulfill the Great Commission.**
The role of the Clans within the tribes of the nation, specific gatherings by blood and allegiance (e.g. house of David) (e.g., the church at Philippi)		
The Ethiopian eunuch, Acts 8	Fight the Good Fight of Faith (FGFF) The Most Amazing Story Ever Told, Bible Blossom, Let God Arise! (LGA) Prayer Resources, TUMI Productions, etc.	Training others how to evangelize and follow up new believers
The Thessalonican believers, 1 and 2 Thess.	FGFF, Heroic Venture, Jesus Cropped from the Picture, Sacred Roots (workshop, book, and resources), Church Year Calendar and Annual, select Foundations courses, SIAFU Chapters and Network, select Ambassadors Workshop courses, Sojourner's Quest, select Capstone modules, LGA Prayer Resources, TUMI Productions, etc.	Training in how to disciple, one on one, small group, connecting with other believers in community, teaching, and providing solid under-shepherding of growing disciples
Timothy, 1 and 2 Tim.	Capstone Curriculum, Ambassadors Workshop Series, Onesimus Workshop, LGA Prayer Resources, Evangel School of Church Planting, TUMI Productions, etc.	Apprentice emerging leaders in particular roles and functions to start new kingdom-oriented ministries, and to strengthen existing ones. We provide the resources and how-to to establish, run, and grow new kingdom-oriented ministries that ultimately will demonstrate the freedom, wholeness, and justice of the Kingdom in and among the poor, at-risk neighborhoods and families (Matt. 13.23).
TUMI works with movements and congregations to establish their own credentialing processes which allow them to certify official agents for ministry.		

APPENDIX 31

Getting a Good Team Rhythm:
Time Management and Ministry Stewardship
Rev. Dr. Don L. Davis

Basic Theological Assumptions

- The Kingdom of God is the framework of all ministry.
- The Church is both foretaste and agent of the Kingdom of God.
- Through our witness and actions we proclaim Christ's reign through the Church to the world.
- As a Team, we are to seek God's face regarding our ministry endeavors and strive to accomplish them efficiently and excellently.
- God desires his people to be wise in their proclamation of the Kingdom.

Ministry Management Strategy

I. Clarify Your Identity and Mission

  A. What is our ultimate purpose and identity?

  B. What are our key ministry areas (worship, witness, learning, mission, justice, service)?

  C. What are our ultimate commitments (to God in Christ, to Scripture, to the Church, to the world)?

  D. What are our ultimate convictions, ideals, and values?

II. Understand Your Particular Field of Mission

  A. What is the history of our particular field of mission?

  B. For whom and to whom are our efforts directed?

  C. What are the critical needs, and how are they currently being met?

  D. What programs/activities currently exist to meet them?

  E. How effective have they been to alleviate these needs?

  F. What conditions currently demand attention or relief?

Getting a Good Team Rhythm: Time Management and Ministry Stewardship, continued

III. Appraise Your Resources (Situational Analysis)

A. What is the level of our commitment and burden to this need?

B. Who is currently working on these problems or available to work (people and personnel)?

C. What facilities, equipment, and materials do we have?

D. What kind of budget and monies do we currently have?

E. What training or preparation do we offer?

F. What factors help (opportunities) or hinder (threats) us in seeking to address these needs?

IV. Formulate Goals to Meet Needs

A. Set a planning cycle (six months to one year is recommended).

B. State your goals in terms of one clear statement and idea (clarity).

C. Make certain that your goals are able to be done (feasibility).

D. State your goals in terms of end results: how much and how many (Specificity).

    1. How many (number)?

    2. How well done (quality)?

    3. How much (quantity)?

E. Determine how long or what date you expect these to take place.

V. Establish Clear Priorities

A. Does this goal relate to our ultimate purposes and objectives?

B. Of all possible goals, which are most important to us now?

C. Of the important goals, which ones must be done immediately?

D. Of the important goals, which ones should be done sometime soon?

E. Which goals ought to be postponed for later consideration?

VI. Determine Plans and Strategies

A. Outline step-by-step strategies for each important goal.

B. What precisely are the steps and phases for this project?

C. What specific courses of action does this project require?

D. Who is responsible for this project (for what, for whom, to whom)?

E. What training will the participants require, and where will they obtain it?

F. What resources do we need, and how will we get it (people, money, facilities, equipment, training, counsel)?

VII. Execute Your Plans according to Schedule

A. Create a project schedule.

B. Communicate to all parties their roles and responsibilities.

C. Coordinate activities at appropriate times.

D. Set dates for review and feedback.

E. Set up appointments for accountability, review, and assessment.

VIII. Review and Evaluate Effectiveness in Light of Goals

A. What did we hope to accomplish?

B. Did we accomplish our goals? Why or why not?

C. Should this or another goal be repeated? Why or why not?

D. How did those responsible perform?

E. Did these efforts bring us any closer to our ultimate goal, or did these activities deter and distract us?

IX. Revise Goals, Priorities, and Strategies for New Cycle

Use information received to assess needs more clearly, to set better goals, formulate better strategies, and obtain better results for the glory of God.

APPENDIX 32

Theological Diversity

Rev. Dr. Don L. Davis

I. The Importance of Theology

A. It is critical to credible faith: Rom. 10.17 – So faith comes from hearing, and hearing through the word of Christ.

B. It is critical to apostolic community: Jude 1.3-4 – Beloved, although I was very eager to write to you about our common salvation, I found it necessary to write appealing to you to contend for the faith that was once for all delivered to the saints. [4] For certain people have crept in unnoticed who long ago were designated for this condemnation, ungodly people, who pervert the grace of our God into sensuality and deny our only Master and Lord, Jesus Christ.

C. It is critical to godly leadership: Titus 1.9 – He must hold firm to the trustworthy word as taught, so that he may be able to give instruction in sound doctrine and also to rebuke those who contradict it.

II. The Reality of Diversity in Christian Traditions

A. We are diverse in our *patterns of religious authority*: how we make decisions and recognize rulership.

B. We are diverse in our *hermeneutical methods*: how we read and interpret the Scriptures.

C. We are diverse in our *lived traditions*: how we worship and serve the same Lord of all.

III. The Essential Rule of Faith: The Nicene Creed

A. The Vincentian Rule of theological conviction: "All possible care must be taken that we hold that faith which has been believed everywhere, always, and by all" (Vincent of Lerins, "A Commonitory," *Nicene and post-Nicene Fathers*).

B. The significance of the Creed: concise summary of the essentials

In the history of the church, the Nicene Creed has been the key statement of what is essential to Christian belief.

1. *Augustine* [says about the creeds]: Let thing content with thing, cause with cause, reason with reason on the authority of Scripture, an authority not peculiar to either, but common to all. In this way, councils would be duly respected, and yet the highest place would be given to Scripture, every thing being brought to it as a test.

2. *John Calvin*: Thus those ancient Councils of Nicea, Constantinople, the first of Ephesus, Chalcedon and the like which were held for refuting errors, we willingly embrace, and reverence as sacred, in so far as relates to the doctrines of faith, *for they contain nothing but the pure and genuine interpretation of Scripture*, which the holy Fathers with spiritual prudence adopted to crush the enemies of religion who had then arisen (Institutes IV, ix. 8).

3. *John Wesley*: "John Wesley accorded a fundamental status to the Nicene-Constantinopolitan Creed as both 'a summary of the biblical faith' and as an interpretive web 'for the reading of Scriptures'" (Sen-King Tan, "The Doctrine of the Trinity in John Wesley's Prose and Poetic Works").

C. WI Affirmation of Faith Statement

1. Acknowledgment of the essentials

2. Affirms the "Great Tradition" (ie., theology of the core creedal statements)

3. Asserts the Reformer's central doctrinal claims

4. Addresses post-Nicea doctrinal issues

5. Anchored in broad evangelical perspective

Theological Diversity,
continued

D. The power of inter-denominationality: Peter Meiderlin (Rupertus Meldenius), 17th century Lutheran theologian and pastor

1. In essentials *unity*: Never compromise the Great Tradition, Phil. 2.3; Jude 3.

2. In non-essentials *liberty*: allow for freedom on issues of conscience, Gal. 5.1.

3. In all things *charity*: practice love and charity in everything, John 13.34-35.

E. The problem of dogmatism: "Rabid Theology"

1. Dogmatists alone determine what are "the essentials."

2. Non-essentials do not exist; *all* of their beliefs are essential.

3. They love only those who agree with their view of "the essentials."

IV. Dealing with Disagreements

A. The inevitability of *disagreement*: expect conflict over doctrinal visions

B. The importance of *dialogue*: reason with principled conviction over matters of faith and doctrine

C. The ingredient of *demeanor*: maintain in all things a spirit of charity and respect

D. The importance of *deference*: defer to our denominational partners on non-essentials

Theological Diversity,
continued

V. Conclusions: The Importance of Theological Diversity

In essentials, unity,

in non-essentials, liberty,

in all things, charity.

~ Peter Meiderlin (Rupertus Meldenius),
17th century Lutheran theologian and pastor

We highly recommend watching the video *Theological Diversity*, which can be found at *https://vimeo.com/75492665*

Translation Partnership Agreement SAMPLE
[Language] Capstone Curriculum
[Translation Partner] and The Urban Ministry Institute (TUMI)

June 21, 2019

The Translation Partnership Agreement for [language] Capstone Curriculum (herein referred to as "Contract") states the terms and conditions that govern the contractual agreement between The Urban Ministry Institute of World Impact, Lorna Rasmussen (Chief Project Officer) [herein referred to as "TUMI"] and [Translation Partner ministry]), [Translation Partner representative] [herein referred to as "Translation Partner"] who agrees to this Contract.

1. Terms and Conditions

1. A Translation Partner must first be approved and maintain their status as an official satellite of The Urban Ministry Institute in order for any of the following guidelines to be duly acted upon or carried out.

2. TUMI will provide TUMI's English source files for each resource, one at a time.

3. The Urban Ministry Institute of World Impact, Inc. retains all copyright for the translated materials, and may sell the translated materials to anyone at TUMI's discretion. TUMI/World Impact, Inc. must appear on all translated materials as the copyright holder.

4. The information contained on the copyright page of the translated resource must contain the entire content of the original English language copyright page as well as a translation of the entire English copyright page.

2. Scope of Services

1. TUMI will not be involved in selection of translators or other participants, and TUMI will not have any financial participation in the project.

Translation Partnership Agreement SAMPLE, continued

2. The Translation Partner is responsible to oversee the translation activity. The Translation Partner may hire or engage one or more subcontractors to perform, as they see fit, any of their obligations under this Contract, provided, however, that 1) the Translation Partner shall in all cases remain primarily responsible for all of its obligations under this Contract and 2) the Translation Partner will be responsible to ensure all work done by the subcontractor meets the standards listed within this Contract.

3. The Translation Partner commits to the accurate reproduction of its curricula (i.e., Capstone), adhering strictly to reproducing, without alteration, the substance of its theology, ideas, themes and conclusions.

4. All translators must reproduce the material's meaning using language, grammar, and concepts which provide, as closely as possible, a dynamic equivalence to the meanings taught in the English TUMI curriculum.

5. The translators must translate the material word-for-word, but users should feel free in presenting the modules in a way to fit the contextual needs of the target audience. Translations must strictly follow the actual language included within the curriculum itself. No edits of the material should be undertaken. Teachers and utilizers of the curriculum should feel free to share from their own experience and context to present, highlight, or adapt the materials in their lessons, but the translation must adhere to the language of the text itself.

6. The Translation Partner will report monthly as to progress on Translation until it is completed.

3. Translated Resource

1. The Translation Partner will provide TUMI with the digital files for each resource prior to final production for review, and incorporate edits as necessary.

2. The Translation Partner will provide final files in both InDesign and PDF formats, and shall not be released for publication without TUMI's written approval.

3. TUMI shall have the exclusive right to release the work in any mechanical, electronic, cloud, or other form now known or hereafter invented.

4. TUMI will make each resource available through a widely used platform such as Amazon, Kindle, or Kobo after it has been completed, checked and authorized for release. We will notify the Translation Partner as soon as these are available.

5. The Translation Partners may only re-sell TUMI curriculum (e.g., translated Capstone Student Workbooks) to their students. The translators may not sell any of the translated material to an individual or group outside of their ministry.

6. TUMI permits the Translation Partner to reproduce copies of the translated Student Workbooks for use with its students. The translators must pay TUMI a royalty of 15% of the selling price, with a minimum royalty of $1.00 per book for each translated Student Workbook they reproduce (honor system).

4. Confidentiality

The Translation Partner and any subcontractors hired by the Translation Partner shall not disclose any files or details regarding The Capstone Curriculum quizzes, answer keys, or make copies of any content based on the concepts contained for personal use or for distribution unless requested to do so by TUMI, or use Confidential Information other than solely for the benefit of the Client.

5. No Modification Unless in Writing

No modification of this Contract shall be valid unless in writing and agreed upon by both the Client and Consultant.

Translation Partnership Agreement SAMPLE, continued

6. Dissolution of Contract

If the above contract is breached, The Urban Ministry Institute reserves the right to cancel this contract. Upon cancellation, the translation partner and any of its subcontractors must immediately surrender all source and translated files.

The Urban Ministry Institute and Pursue church agree to this Contract, with the specifics therein.

IN WITNESS WHEREOF:

_____

[Translation Partner representative]
[Translation Partner ministry]

_____

Lorna Rasmussen, Chief Project Officer
The Urban Ministry Institute, World Impact

Date Signed: _____

Date Signed: _____

www.ingramcontent.com/pod-product-compliance
Lightning Source LLC
Chambersburg PA
CBHW081240020426
42331CB00013B/3235